The Wisdom of Statecraft

Sir Herbert Butterfield and the philosophy
of international politics

Alberto R. Coll

Duke University Press

Durham   1985

© 1985 Duke University Press
All rights reserved
Printed in the United States of America

Library of Congress Cataloging in Publication Data
Coll, Alberto R.
The wisdom of statecraft.
Bibliography: p.
Includes index.
1. Butterfield, Herbert, Sir, 1900–
2. International relations—Philosophy.   3. History—
Philosophy.   4. Political science—Philosophy.
I. Title.
D15.B86C65   1985   907'.2024   85-1535
ISBN 0-8223-0607-7

To my mother and father,
who by their example taught
me from the earliest days
the value of ideas

Contents

Prefatory Note

Since its establishment in 1975, the White Burkett Miller Center of Public Affairs, a privately endowed research institution, has sought to advance understanding and scholarship and to improve the structure and functioning of the American Presidency. As part of this task, the Center has played an active role in the development and support of "a new generation of scholars" whose works will have significant impact in addressing the complex domestic and foreign policy challenges facing the nation's highest office.

During the writing of this important work, Alberto Coll was in residence at the Miller Center. He contributed in a major way to its intellectual life. His attention to the broader historical foundations of politics and international relations added another dimension to discussions at Faulkner House. It is a matter of great personal satisfaction and institutional pride that the Miller Center was the home of the research on this highly original book by a brilliant young scholar on the threshold of becoming a leading philosopher of international relations.

Kenneth W. Thompson, Director
White Burkett Miller Center of
Public Affairs
University of Virginia

Foreword

For those of us who knew Sir Herbert Butterfield well and who followed the development of his insights and his judgement over the years, it is profoundly encouraging that an able younger scholar should be able to understand so perceptively what he had to say, for there is no doubt that this is what Alberto Raoul Coll has succeeded in doing. In reaching this conclusion I do not rely on my own judgement alone: Sir Herbert's widow, Lady Butterfield, Professor Kenneth Thompson, and other close friends who have seen the manuscript concur with me. It is therefore unnecessary for me to add anything in this introduction to Professor Coll's lucid and comprehensive analysis. But the reader may be glad to have a personal portrait of the man.

Herbert was a small frail man, untidily dressed and usually in tweeds, hatless in all weathers, and with a shock of untidy hair which gradually grew grayer and whiter but never slicker. He remained as unpretentious and unassuming when he became master of Peterhouse and vice-chancellor of the University and received a knighthood as he had been when, a young don, he drew an immense, packed class of undergraduates from all sorts of faculties to his lectures on modern European history, which he delivered with a spellbinding intensity and with pieces of chalk shaken in his loosely clenched fist like dice in a dice box.

The first of Herbert's traits that come to mind when I think of him is his laughter. He always saw the joke, the irony, in a situation, and he laughed out loud at it. In one way it was like a schoolboy's giggle. If someone took himself too seriously, became a little too dogmatic or pompous, Herbert's eyes would begin to twinkle and his lips to twitch, and if you caught his eye at that moment the joke could be very infectious. There was also an impish, Voltairean quality about his laughter and about his general demeanor. Set against the eternal verities which mattered so much to him, human pretentiousness moved him to ridicule, but even more to puckish amusement. He was fond of Puck's line "Lord, what fools these mortals be"—partly because it gives a more than human dimension to the picture. So too does his often-quoted remark emerging from a meeting at Cambridge which had taken a particularly unfortunate decision: "Won't there be laughter in hell tonight?"

This extrahuman dimension points to a second characteristic of Herbert's. He was a deeply religious man. He was born and grew up in the West Riding of Yorkshire, a bleak land of moorland villages where the Methodist chapel was the source of society and civilization. He retained all his life the loyalties of his childhood, the most important of which was his commitment to Methodism. For many years he preached regularly in Methodist chapels. He took an active interest in the organization and administration of the Methodist church and he never deviated from his Methodist "pledge" to abstain from alcohol, though he served it generously to guests. From his Nonconformity also came his skepticism about the powers that be, about officialdom, about official history above all. Great as was his admiration for Oxford, where he sent his younger son, he would deplore the tendency of too many Oxford dons to "run after Whitehall," to espouse not the lost causes to which that university was once dedicated but the fashionable causes of the day. "I value every one of the fifty two miles that separate Cambridge from Westminster," he would say. With official history he bracketed all partisan history, all exploitation of the past to justify a policy or creed or country in the present. All of it seemed to him, as to many Nonconformists, Erastian, worthy of the vicar of Bray. It offended his uncompromising intellectual integrity, an integrity that was so absolute because he felt it to be a trust from God, never to be rendered unto Caesar. The key part which Herbert's sense of integrity played in his historical writing is admirably explained by Professor Coll, especially with regard to the Whig interpretation of history.

But the rich civilization of Cambridge and the immense diversity of the past which Herbert strove so hard to recapture as it really was made him increasingly conscious of the significance of Jesus' teaching that His Father's house has many mansions. Methodism, and the example of the Wesleys, was his mansion (John Wesley was born less than a hundred miles from Herbert, and he died less than a hundred years before Herbert was born). But his intellectual and spiritual insight alike drew back from the conceit that his mansion was closer to God than those of others. In many conversations he would say that all the sects into which the Western Church became fragmented at the Reformation and since, were derived from the Latin Christendom of the Middle Ages. He looked back beyond medieval Christendom to Augustine, and his approach to history and to life was deeply Augustinian. He attended Church of England services in his College chapel and elsewhere, sometimes with me. Increasingly also he became aware of the spiritual values of Roman Catholicism. For this understanding, he owed much to his lifelong study of the Catholic historian Acton and to his friendship with Dom David Knowles, also of Peterhouse and an outstanding Catholic medieval scholar. Herbert felt honored that the Catholic university system of Ireland invited him to be its external examiner in history, of all sensitive subjects. He accepted without difficulty, almost as an enlargement of his own personality, the decision of his eldest son Peter to become a Catholic and to live in Dublin. He was also much attracted by traditional Judaism, especially its championship of religious values against courts and kings.

But this breadth of awareness remained spiritual, a sympathy for others who also reached out to a transcendent God. I never found in him much sympathy for the Madonna, and he was puzzled that I should see value in popular Hindu beliefs. For him all such devotion amounted to "mere nature-worship," the idolatry of created things rather than their Creator. He remained, in the splendid line of the Ulster poet Louis MacNeice, "Banned for ever from the candles of the Irish poor." Even more he disliked the worship of texts, of scripture written and selected and copied by fallible men. "No image worship," he liked to say, "has ever led to half so much error, or half so much human suffering, as the worship of the written word." With his historian's scorn for biblical literalism, an attitude which he considered "beneath serious discussion," went his distrust of the blind belief in reason or progress. For him it was all of a piece—"bowing down to sticks and stones and abstract nouns," as he said with his impish grin.

Herbert was strongly attracted by harmony. Though nobody could argue a case more tenaciously than he, he insisted that the historian must not take sides or identify himself with one of the participants in a struggle, but rather maintain an equal understanding of them all, however bitterly they fought each other. Above all the historian must learn to see how "the next stage in the story" was the product not of the victory of one side but of the very conflict itself. This search for the wider harmonies that reconciled conflicting themes, and a natural sensitivity of the ear, led him to find solace in music and in poetry rather than in the visual arts which so appealed to his wife. I remember him sitting long hours at the piano, playing to himself until the music relaxed the tensions that had built up in him and restored his peace of mind. His favorite poets were intellectual, like Valery, and portrayers of a meaningful universe, like Dante. Dante he especially loved. He had a pocket edition of the *Divina Commedia*, the volumes of which looked like prayer books, and he often took one to chapel, to read if the sermon became too platitudinous. The harmonies of the poetry itself appealed to him as much as the immense, detailed order of the cosmogony. His belief that the whole intricate web of creation reflects the nature of its Creator is most limpidly expressed by Beatrice in the first canto of the *Paradiso*:

Le cose tutte a quante
Han ordine tra loro; e questo e forma
Che l'universo a Dio fa simigliante.

(All things that exist have an order linking them; and it is this pattern which makes the universe similar to God.)

Herbert was very much a Yorkshireman—what others in the north of England call a tyke, a breed that takes some measuring up to; and he was English, in the same matter-of-fact way that he was a Methodist, without chauvinism and without regret. He did not go abroad, as some Englishmen do, to escape from England or himself; it was simply that in the north of Italy and in Ireland he felt well and worked well. He was especially fond of Venice and of the Italian lakes. He said that he did his best work at the Villa Serbelloni on Lake Como, maintained for the use of scholars by the Rockefeller Foundation. He loved Italian history and perhaps for that reason he disliked romantic sentimentality about the Italian past. "I am as fond of modern Italy as I am of Machiavelli's."

The range of Herbert's historical writing is unusually wide, as Alberto Coll shows—from the broad multilingual panorama of manuscripts and notes on *The Origins of History* (which it fell to me to edit after his death) to detailed reconstruction of specific events like Napoleon's peace tactics in 1808. He was interested in the history of science, the history of ideas, and the history of history itself as a conscious way of coming to terms with the past. He appreciated the value of social and economic history, which provide us with the context in which events happened and men made decisions. But he saw them as parts, indeed subordinate parts, of the whole process of reconstruction of the past. "Those who build up their outlook only from the social sciences," he wrote in the *Dictionary of the History of Ideas*, "will have only a sectionalized view of the overall process of historical change, a process in which the genius of a single leader who sees and uses existing conditions can secure an enormous leverage, and a handful of men who have faith can move mountains. . . . It is possible that democracy will also radically turn its back on what was for so long a main objective in historical writing—the communication of what the art of statesmanship requires." It was important to be scrupulously honest with the facts and to discover them by detailed research, not in order to amass a great heap of formless sawdust but in order to distill from them the wisdom that will enable us to understand public affairs. Wisdom for him was derived from conscious reflection about the wealth of accumulated experience that enables statesmen, and indeed all who have a hand in the political process, to govern well. Louis Bouyer states that "Wisdom is the art of living based on experience, and above all a tradition of experience criticized by rational reflection." Alberto Coll is profoundly right to call this book *The Wisdom of Statecraft*.

Political wisdom seemed to Herbert particularly necessary in the conduct of international affairs, and this is one of the principal reasons for his special interest in that field. Inside a single state, rival theories and partisan struggles were usually concerned with how the polity as a whole should be governed. On the other hand, statesmen who conducted the foreign policy of an independent member of the patchwork quilt that made up the European states system acted to protect and promote the interests of only one element in the whole. Yet they also had to act, collectively, to preserve the system itself, which brought advantages to all its members. Statesmanship in the international sphere required the recognition of this wider responsibility, as well as the skill and judgement needed to obtain advantages for one's own state within the system. In the international field, Herbert held, a statesman needs awareness of the lessons of experience, restraint in pursuing state interests, and an ethical sense of what is publicly right—which for him was different but no less binding than the private ethics of an individual. He attached importance to the maxims of statesmanship derived from experience—maxims such as "never drive the enemy into a corner from which he cannot easily retreat" and "remember that you may need the enemy of today as an ally tomorrow." His interest in international relations was excited by the operating skills of individual statesmen—not so much negotiating ability as a flair for recognizing opportunity and for taking it promptly, an elastic realism, and a strategic perceptiveness—as well as by the moral dimension of statecraft. He was particularly interested in Richelieu, whose achievement stands out in both respects; in the two parallel diplomacies of Louis XIV; in Metternich's and Bismarck's management of the precarious balance; and in Napoleon, who was the great master of realistic opportunism but had no sense of moral responsibility towards the system. The clearest expression of Herbert's mature thought on this subject is set out in his address on raison d'état, delivered in memory of Martin Wight, his closest academic partner in international history.

But Herbert's interest in individual statesmen and in the rules of successful statecraft was ancillary to his principal aim, which was to achieve a view of the states-system as a whole. It is on this aim, and on the degree to which Herbert achieved it, that Professor Coll focuses our attention and which he expounds and illuminates most effectively. Like Herbert, Alberto Coll is attracted to statesmen who saw the game in all its complexity and in its moral as well as its strategic dimension. He shows how Herbert's concept of diplomacy reflected his sense of balance, his search for an overarching harmony and purpose. For Herbert tried to see the states-system as Beatrice saw the universe, or as Goethe saw it when he exclaimed, "Wie alles sich zum

Ganzen webt, Eins in das andere wirbt und strebt!" (How everything weaves itself into a whole, and one thing works and pushes its way into the other!) The workings of the system and what this book calls the philosophy of international politics could only emerge, Herbert believed, from the source of events themselves. For him history remained *una storia*, and the detective work of the historian ought finally to result in a revised and more meaningful narrative, from which the principles of statesmanship and the wisdom of history could be learned. As he and Martin Wight put it in their preface to *Diplomatic Investigations*, "The underlying aim of the present collection is to clarify the principles of prudence and moral obligation which have held together the international society of states throughout its history, and still hold it together." This book clarifies those principles, as well as Herbert's contribution to our understanding of them.

Those were the objectives which Herbert kept before the British Committee on the Theory of International Politics. He founded and was the first chairman of this small and private group of scholars and practitioners, and he continued to dominate it after Martin Wight, and then I, took over the chair. The impact of his ideas and interests is clearly visible over the years, not only in the academic members of the committee like Martin Wight, Michael Howard, Hedley Bull, and Kenneth Thompson, but also in the practitioners, notably Noel Dorr, at present Irish Representative on the United Nations Security Council, and Sir Robert Wade-Gery, at present British High Commissioner in India.

Professor Coll has set out for us in this book, with great skill and sensitivity, the historical, political, and religious aspects of Herbert Butterfield's thought and writing. It is the best and the most accurate exposition I know of the contribution of a man who ranks with the greatest of the long line of Cambridge historians—as has been aptly said, beside Macaulay, Acton, and Trevelyan. By making Herbert's thought accessible in this way, Professor Coll has rendered the thoughtful reading public here and in Britain, as well as scholars and students, a signal service. Professor John Clive of Harvard concluded his admirable essay on Herbert in *The New Republic* with the words: "It is hard to believe that *The Origins of History* is Butterfield's last book. Whether we always agree with him or not, we shall miss his searching intelligence, his knack for asking the hard questions, his quiet tone of voice and his thoughtful pen." Alberto Coll's book will do much to insure that Herbert Butterfield's quiet, honest, searching mind remains with us.

Adam Watson
Center for Advanced Studies
University of Virginia

Preface

My initial impetus for undertaking this work several years ago was my love of three related disciplines, history, politics, and theology, and the hope that in studying the thought of someone who had so well blended these I might be assisted in my own search for a coherent synthesis. Not only was this hope amply fulfilled, but in the course of reading and studying Sir Herbert Butterfield I was also inspired by his virtues of mind and character, especially his profound humility, his intellectual openness and catholicity, and his quiet but firm refusal to confuse transcendental truth with relative judgments—the persistent affirmation of the distinction, so important to political discourse and action, between the City of God and the City of Man. In a very personal sense, I owe a tremendous debt of gratitude to Butterfield for such inspiration.

I also owe much more than I can ever express to my teachers at Princeton University and the University of Virginia. Intellectually and morally, Kenneth W. Thompson has been a mentor and kind friend. His persistent and sometimes severe admonitions to personal discipline and concentration in the pursuit of scholarship and his innumerable acts of faithfulness, kindness, and generosity are marks of a great man who cares for his students. Without him this book would not have been written. Adam Watson also provided warm encouragement and sound guidance as I worked on the doctoral dissertation out of which this book originated. He facilitated access, with the kind permission of Lady Butterfield, to several of Butterfield's manuscripts which to this day remain unpublished, and he always had a flair for pointing out to me those nuances and subtleties of Butterfield's thought that I had missed. Professors Enno Kraehe, Norman Graebner, and Calvin Woodard offered helpful suggestions at the formative stages of the manuscript. There are others who, in a less direct fashion, played a very important role in the process which led to this work: Inis L. Claude, Jr., through his own writings and his example of scholarly excellence and intellectual integrity; Whittle Johnston, whose stimulating lectures on the theory of international relations during my first semester of graduate study awoke within me a tremendous surge of curiosity and enthusiasm for the subject; and Dante Germino, through his love of political philosophy.

In the research and writing of the various drafts of this book I received generous financial assistance from several private foundations. The Charlotte W. Newcombe Foundation provided a fellowship which enabled me to spend a full year on the research and writing of the doctoral dissertation. The Danforth-Compton foundation awarded me a substantial research grant for the year 1982–83, and the Institute for the Study of World Politics awarded a generous summer grant for 1983. They made it possible to turn the dissertation into this book. At the White Burkett Miller Center of Public Affairs of the University of Virginia, where many of the seeds for the work were first planted, I found a warm and friendly scholarly community supportive of my endeavors, as I also have found among my colleagues at the Department of Government of Georgetown University, where I am privileged to teach.

Mr. Christopher Lamb of Georgetown University read the entire manuscript with a highly critical eye. For his valuable comments and his inspiring friendship, I am most grateful. The Provost and Vice-President for Academic Affairs of Georgetown University, Rev. J. Donald Freeze, S.J., kindly provided funds for the preparation of the index. Mrs. Bettie Hall of the University of Virginia and Sandra Rosenberg of the Department of Government of Georgetown were very patient and helpful as they typed the manuscript's drafts. A word of thanks is also due to the editors of the Duke University Press, especially Mr. Reynolds Smith.

It will be of interest to some readers of this book that Butterfield was very fond of Duke University, having spent some time there during the spring of 1969 as a visiting scholar. This was right in the aftermath of some of the worst student disturbances that shook the United States, to which Duke was no exception. Shortly before Sir Herbert and Lady Butterfield arrived on campus, the students had invaded and occupied the president's lodging for several days. Not surprisingly, during his short visit Sir Herbert did his best, in a quiet and unobtrusive way, to help bring back to the university that atmosphere of civility, reasonableness, and toleration which he treasured. In addition to giving some lectures on the subject of history and historical criticism, he conducted one or two graduate seminars. The Butterfields enjoyed becoming acquainted with the president and some of the faculty, including Professors Petrie, Gunter, and Parker, and Professor Frank Baker of the Divinity School. They also enjoyed immensely the beautiful flower gardens and the magnificent chapel with its music and large congregation.

The list of all those who, through their friendship and kindness, have contributed to this book in more ways than they imagine, is too long to recite here. But it must include Mr. Luis V. Manrara, with whom I have been privileged to carry out a dialogue on the great issues of politics and society for the last fourteen years; Ernest Gordon, whose magnificent sermons at the Princeton University Chapel moved me with excitement toward the great intellectual heritage of the Church throughout the ages; and James M. Houston, whose life has been a beautiful example of service and integrity of character. Finally, I must mention my dear wife, Nancy, whose patience, loving affection, and quiet virtues have been a source of strength and refreshment in a tumultuous world.

I

The Sources of Political Wisdom

If history is ever to help us to solve even an infinitesimal part of the great and grievous riddle of life, we must quit the regions of personal and temporal foreboding for a sphere in which our view is not forthwith dimmed by self. It may be that a calmer consideration from a greater distance may yield a first hint of the true nature of life on earth.

Jacob Burckhardt,
Reflections on History

1

Sir Herbert Butterfield:
The historian, the political thinker,
and the Christian

In a world that often seems poised on the brink of nuclear war and economic catastrophe, few would deny the need for enlightenment from any source that can assist citizens and statesmen in conceiving and carrying out a foreign policy suitable for the challenges at hand. Statecraft in the international dimensions with which this essay is concerned, the political, diplomatic, and military intercourse among states, carries upon its frail shoulders moral and historical responsibilities of an awesome character. The need for wisdom in statecraft never has been greater or more urgent.

Two explanatory notes at the outset of this book, one concerning the title, the other the author's underlying assumptions, seem appropriate. This is a study of Sir Herbert Butterfield's contributions to the study and understanding of international politics. The use of the term "the philosophy of international politics" does not imply that there is only one approach or one way of analyzing the subject; it refers instead to that body of intellectual inquiry, much of it philosophical in nature, which is devoted to the political relations among states and nations throughout the course of human history.

Although this is largely a presentation of Butterfield's ideas and their implications, some of the writer's own judgments and points of interpretation are evident, as they inevitably must be in any work on political philosophy. The intellectual assumptions on which the author's analysis rests are similar to Butterfield's: the truth of biblical Christianity; the enduring relevance of that broad and ancient intellectual tradition known as political realism, represented in modern American life by such well-known figures as Reinhold Niebuhr and Hans Morgenthau; and a belief in the importance of understanding the past if one is to manage with a limited degree of success the complexities of the present. It is possible from these three general assumptions to arrive at specific conclusions different from those reached by Butterfield or the author, as it is also possible to read Butterfield's work and arrive at some particular interpretations different from those in this book. Nevertheless, the assumptions are set out here for the sake of clarity and intellectual integrity. Throughout this work, I have tried to do as little violence to Butterfield's ideas as possible. Although I have felt free to criticize Butterfield on some issues, my main task has been the exposition and elaboration of his ideas rather than mine, so that each reader may be able to conduct his own dialogue with Butterfield and reach his own conclusions.

Any probings of Sir Herbert Butterfield's conception of wisdom in statecraft must address his definition of wisdom. Butterfield himself never made a systematic attempt to offer such a definition; instead, he seems to have assumed that the definition would gradually emerge and take living substance in the course of his explorations of history, politics, and Christianity.[1] Rather than start out with an abstract pronouncement of what wise statecraft was and measuring all historical reality by that standard, Butterfield followed an approach more suitable to his historical method. This approach consisted of studying first the actual practice of international politics in different periods—he placed heavy emphasis on modern European history since 1492—analyzing its theoretical foundations and its consequences in the world of historical events, and then searching for those models of statecraft which seemed to have produced the best results and which contained sufficient relevance for the student and practitioner of twentieth-century international relations.

A reference to best results immediately raises the question of values, of the normative standards by which Butterfield, after allowing history to display its rich diversity of approaches to the moral and political dilemmas of statesmanship, evaluated some approaches as preferable to others. These standards, which jointly constituted Butterfield's implicit definition of wisdom, were derived from the rich heritage of Western civilization, and it is worthwhile to present an outline of them at the beginning of this work.

In today's world, the great questions of statecraft are confronted in the full range of what Max Weber called "the ethics of responsibility" by the leaders of individual nation-states. For all the attention lavished on them by contemporary social scientists, the decision makers of transnational entities or of major domestic groups have neither the power, the weight of legitimacy, the representational capacity, nor the broad spectrum of awesome moral choices in foreign policy which the leaders of nation-states generally have. It is with reference to the last, therefore, that Butterfield's definition of wisdom acquires substance.

For Butterfield, wise statecraft had two simultaneous goals: the protection of the people under the statesman's care and the nurture of a system of international relations in which the pursuit of survival and prosperity by other states could be harmonized with one's own pursuit and everyone else's. Foreign policy had to take into account the requirements of the national interest without unduly neglecting those of international order. Each of these poles of obligation had its distinct set of demands; in its finest moments, statecraft tried to reduce the tension between the poles and widen the settings in which solicitude for international order served the national interest and vice versa. What was foolish for the statesman to do, however, at least in the international system of the twentieth century and in the European one of the previous four centuries, was to promote one set of requirements by undermining or ignoring the other set, to turn the creative and sometimes incandescent friction between the national interest and international order into a zero-sum game, in which one pole eclipsed the other completely. The pursuit of world dominion, or the total surrender of one's political and cultural integrity as represented and protected by state independence, was for Butterfield a destructive pattern of statecraft.

International order, which Butterfield described as a system of international relations in which violent conflict among member states was generally regulated and limited so as to protect every state against the loss of its independence, was a morally worthy objective. The moral worth of international order and state independence rested on several grounds. First, states were the most effective units of political organization throughout the world community, and there were few signs that they would not remain so for the foreseeable future. Efforts to reduce violence and to promote the stability necessary for the development of a humane civilization had to be mediated through the state; to abolish the state and to refashion the political framework underlying international relations accordingly were tasks likely to produce far greater chaos and destruction than those generated by the present state-system. Second, in true Rankean fashion, Butterfield believed that by encouraging cultural and political individuation within many different political communities the state-system served an additional moral purpose; the advocates of a world state had addressed very inadequately the problems of uniformity, centralization, and totalitarianism that might be spawned by the concentration of all world political and military power in a single entity.

The means of foreign policy were also an important component of Butterfield's conception of wise statecraft. Such means could not be divorced from either moral guideposts or the living realities of politics. The norms which Butterfield thought applicable to politics were not exactly those which the Christian ethic enjoined every person to follow. In politics norms played a more modest, more circumscribed role than in the life of the individual; the ethics of limitation supplanted the ethics of aspiration. The regulation of violence and the maintenance of limited stability and order were often the highest ethical objectives a statesman could achieve in the fragmentary, fallen condition of world politics.

Whereas it was possible for an individual to do the good for its own sake along the lines of Kant's imperative, in the foreign policy of states morality could succeed only when it was allied with self-interest, when it paid tangible rewards. Hence, the balance of power, diplomacy, and the pursuit of a rudimentary international order were generally far wiser and more effective instruments of statecraft than other more ambitious means of transforming international relations.

In rating the management of conflict, a more important task of statecraft than its abolition, Butterfield was implicitly following the dominant political tradition of the West, as represented by Augustine, Aquinas, and Grotius. Butterfield was well acquainted with and indebted to the first and last of these. With regards to Aquinas, Butterfield was familiar with his writings and those of his successors on the just war, and he especially cherished those aspects of the Catholic just war tradition dealing with the *ius in bello* and the importance of moderation in warfare.[2] Interestingly, Augustine, Aquinas, and Grotius also thought that the division of the world into various independent states was a moral good, preferable at any rate to the dangers of world tyranny and the ravages of war for global conquest.

While he eschewed the utopianism, globalism, and pacifism prevalent in much of twentieth-century thinking, Butterfield adhered to the standards of moral reasonableness prescribed for statecraft by the Western tradition with which he associated himself. His Grotian abhorrence of acts of unspeakable inhumanity or wanton destruction; his insistence that the statesman maintain the distinction between the people and the government in the conduct of war and diplomacy with adversary states; his Burkean counsels to political forgiveness and generosity; his warnings against national self-righteousness and against the pursuit of wars with unlimited means and unlimited objectives; and his plea to the statesman to remember that original sin is not the sole possession of the enemy were essential ingredients of Butterfield's conception of wise statecraft. Their inclusion suggested that, while Christianity and the great moral tradition of the West could not fully liberate the conduct of foreign policy from its tragic boundaries, they nevertheless could provide far more illumination and opportunities for creative moral action than the cynics might claim.

The insights into international politics of an eminent Christian historian can hardly be dismissed as irrelevant by students or practitioners of the subject. While it is possible to disagree with Butterfield on numerous issues, it is much more difficult to argue that his reflections on the contribution of Christianity to international relations, his probings of the relationship of historical thinking to the conduct of foreign affairs, or his wrestlings with the problems of politics, power, and diplomacy should not be regarded as an important twentieth-century contribution to the ongoing dialogue on these issues which has been an integral part of the political and intellectual life of Western civilization since its earliest days.

Concerning his own work, Butterfield would have made the same warning he issued regarding the study of history. It is not a manual of particular choices or policies which the statesman can consult and follow to the letter in every situation that confronts him; rather it is a body of ideas which he ought to keep in the back of his mind as he goes about his daily tasks, a series of observations about the processes of time and the workings of politics intended to enrich and broaden, not dictate, the statesman's judgment. To use Edmund Burke's felicitous description of the proper role of history in statesmanship, it is valuable as habit, not as precept. His ideas foster a more flexible, less willful attitude toward the processes of time, a more catholic understanding of the knotty moral dilemmas in international relations and the means with which to face them. So it may be that a reading of Butterfield's works can have its most lasting and salutary impact on one's general approach or way of thinking, on the whole series of intangible emotive and rational considerations that determine our political decisions more than we care to admit.

The unassuming man who was to become Regius Professor of Modern History and vice-chancellor of Cambridge University was born into a devout Methodist family in the Yorkshire village of Oxenhope, a few miles south of the Brontes' Haworth, on October 7, 1900. His mother was a member of the Plymouth Brethren. His father, who left school at the age of ten because of his own father's death, had been unable to fulfill his ambition of becoming a Methodist minister and worked as a clerk in a Keighley wool mill. One of Butterfield's friends has commented that "among the fascinating things about him, this was preeminent, that though he came to possess one of the most far-ranging minds, he gave no sensation whatever that he reacted against his beginning. He retained the simplicity, a touch at times of the austerity, and always the loyalties of his childhood."[3]

The most important formative influence on Butterfield's character and religious faith was his father and the very intimate relationship which father and son developed:

> From about age seven or eight until age fourteen he and his father walked together often in the evening. As he remembers it, his father would talk—about nature, his ambitions, God, faith, something they had read. He spoke quietly and stated his views almost like a confession of faith. Herbert loved these walks and was devoted to his father. He compares his father's influence to that of Jesuits over the young in former days. Herbert's mother dominated the household and sometimes seemed to regard his father as rather

weak. Herbert, however, saw his father as a very powerful man, and he submitted himself to his father's influence. It might be fair to say that his father became the religious and personal touchstone in his life, and it was chiefly these walks that made him so.[4]

In 1919, after attending the Trade and Grammar School at Keighley, Butterfield won a scholarship to Peterhouse, the oldest college in Cambridge University and traditionally a strong center of historical learning. His tutor was Paul Vellacott, his main mentor the eminent diplomatic historian Harold Temperley, from whom Butterfield received rigorous training in the methods of historical research. Temperley also introduced Butterfield to the writings of two great historians who had the most profound influence on Butterfield's work: Leopold von Ranke and Lord Acton. In 1923, Butterfield himself became a fellow of Peterhouse.

Early in his scholarly career, Butterfield became concerned with three aspects of historical science that engaged his attention recurrently throughout his life. These were the methods and purposes of narrative history, the role of the imagination in the recreation of the past, and the relationship of the historian's philosophical assumptions to his historical researches. Butterfield was highly conscious of the centrality which the narration of events and the actions of personalities should occupy in historical writing. The Italian word for history, *storia*, expressed the idea that history was above all the telling of a story, the portrayal of a series of events which had its own thematic integrity and upon which the historian or storyteller should not impose his own preconceived notions of direction and meaning. Narrative history in all its richness of detail and unpredictability was the historian's chief business, as well as the indispensable foundation for any subsequent generalizations or abstractions. The accurate telling of the story had to precede the interpretation of it. Butterfield applied these ideas successfully in *The Peace Tactics of Napoleon, 1806–1808* (1929), which he wrote with Temperley's encouragement, and which combined literary gracefulness with a masterful understanding and exposition of the individual personalities of the statesmen involved and of the variegated consequences of their actions.

Earlier, in 1924, Butterfield had written *The Historical Novel*, his first book, pointing to the necessity of cultivating the skills of the imagination if the historian hoped to avoid the anachronistic fallacy of seeing the past through the eyes of contemporary values and categories. Narrative history could succeed only if the historian retold the story as it actually happened, as it interacted with and was shaped by the personalities, actions, and perceptions of those who participated in it. This preoccupation with transcending the historian's cultural and ideological perspective—with putting oneself in the place of others through a mighty exercise of sympathetic imagination, understanding, a suspension of judgment, and ultimately Christian love—would bear fruit later in Butterfield's analyses of diplomacy and his prescriptions to statesmen.

The course charted by these first two works led to *The Whig Interpretation of History* (1931), which established Butterfield's scholarly reputation as a historian throughout the Western world. In this essay Butterfield criticized the tendency of what he called the Whig historian to allow his philosophical and political assumptions to dominate the direction and conclusions of his research. The question of the place which the historian's presuppositions should have in his work troubled Butterfield all his life. Like the rest of his colleagues and predecessors, he never answered it to full satisfaction, but he deserves credit for the meticulousness with which he pointed to the inescapability of assumptions, the subtlety and tenacity of the historian's bias, and the simultaneous need and even partial feasibility of reducing the scope of these to give to *storia* at least a fair opportunity for asserting its inner integrity.

Although they overlap in many respects, Butterfield's works can be divided into four general categories. First are his works of narrative history, upon which his standing as a professional historian rests most strongly. Although they reveal much about Butterfield's mind and are of great value to the student of history, their relevance to the philosophy of international politics is mostly indirect; an adequate treatment of them is outside the scope of this essay. In addition to *The Peace Tactics of Napoleon*, they include a shorter biography of the French genius, *Napoleon* (1939), in which Butterfield surprisingly said very little about the political or philosophical implications of Bonaparte's statecraft, focusing instead on Napoleon as a man; his researches on the transition from aristocratic to democratic government in eighteenth-century England, which took the shape of the celebrated study *George III, Lord North, and the People, 1779–1780* (1949), and a book on Charles James Fox for which he did much work but which he never completed; and his pioneering work, *The Origins of Modern Science* (1949), which has sold more copies than any other of his writings and which did much to establish the history of science as a separate discipline. These are essentially works of pure historical narration.

Butterfield the interpreter surfaces most strongly in the other three groups of writings: those on the history of historiography, on diplomacy and statecraft, and on Christianity. Although long parts of the history of historiography are essentially narrative, much of it also deals with philosophical questions that revolve around the issue of man's attitudes towards the processes of time and the consequences of such attitudes for political institutions, as well as for historical writing itself. Butterfield's efforts in this field were among his most significant services to historical scholarship. Alongside the youthful *Historical Novel* and the more mature *Whig Interpretation of History* were *The Englishman and His History* (1944), a study of the impact which historical thinking and a series of interpretations of the English historical heritage had on the political thought and practice of the late seventeenth-century Whigs; *Man on His Past* (1955), which deals with the development of historiography in the eighteenth and nineteenth centuries, particularly the historical methodology of Lord Acton and Leopold von Ranke; *George III and the Historians* (1957), a reassessment of various historical interpretations of George III's reign which also demonstrated the impact assumptions derived implicitly or explicitly from political theory can have on the historian's work. Finally, there were the Gifford Lectures which Butterfield gave in 1965 and 1966, a mighty attempt to survey the entire history of historiography from man's earliest beginnings to the eighteenth century, the point from which *Man on His Past* started. Although they spanned the ancient civilizations of the East as well as the West, the lectures seemed to Butterfield an incomplete treatment of the subject in many ways; his efforts to revise and expand them having been frustrated by ill health and his many other commitments, the lectures were published posthumously, thanks to the editing skills of Butterfield's good friend Adam Watson, under the title *The Origins of History* (1981).

The Statecraft of Machiavelli (1940) was Butterfield's first major foray into political theory and the relation of statecraft to ethics. Significantly, the first half of this work was a discussion of the influence played by Machiavelli's views of history on his philosophy of statecraft. World War II and the subsequent cold war between the Soviet Union and the Western Alliance intensified Butterfield's concern with the problems of international politics, leading to the publication of *Christianity, Diplomacy and War* (1953) and *International Conflict in the Twentieth Century: A Christian View* (1960).

In 1958, with funding and encouragement from the Rockefeller Foundation and its vice-president, Kenneth W. Thompson, who was Butterfield's closest friend and warmest admirer on this side of the Atlantic, Butterfield founded the British Committee on the Theory of International Politics. This study group, which Butterfield chaired over a decade, included the historians Martin Wight, Michael Howard, and Desmond Williams; the philosopher Donald MacKinnon; the political scientist Hedley Bull; and a small number of government officials, among them the diplomat Adam Watson. The committee had a profound influence on Butterfield's thinking; in the various papers he prepared for its discussions, one can find numerous valuable insights into the problems of statecraft and international relations, insights that later found their way into published essays such as those in *Diplomatic Investigations* (1966). Concerning the significance of the British Committee and of Butterfield's involvement in it, Kenneth W. Thompson has written:

The British approach was the antithesis of that of flourishing schools in America and Australia that dealt with international relations theory and systems analysis. Its frame of reference was the conduct of diplomacy, international society, and the nation-state system. Its point of view was historical, empirical and deductive. Its underlying presuppositions assumed that historical continuities were more important than innovations in the international system; that statecraft provided an historical deposit of accumulated practical wisdom; that the classical writers in politics, diplomacy and law had not been superseded by recent findings in such disciplines as psychology and sociology; and that the corpus of earlier diplomatic and military experience was worthy of study and reformulation to meet contemporary needs.[5]

Underlying Butterfield's understanding of international politics was a severe Christian realism, the fruit of his deep Christian faith. Christianity was the center of his life, and he never ceased to probe its implications for the world of politics and for the study of history. Next to *The Origins of Modern Science*, his most widely read book remains *Christianity and History* (1949). The Methodist form of his faith, in which the Wesleyan reminder, "There, but for the grace of God, go I" played a central role, made him highly conscious of the perils of self-righteousness in his own life as well as in the life of nations. From Methodism he also acquired a mildly critical attitude towards institutional Christianity, especially towards any alliance by the Church with power and its coercive methods.

There was a sense in which Butterfield's transcendent loyalties made him unable ultimately to take politics too seriously. He was, of course, an avid student of international relations, and he invested much agony and effort in proposing creative approaches to the problems of foreign affairs. But, as the word "approach" suggests, he never thought there could be any permanent solutions, only temporary and highly relative ones. The earnest quest for Utopia seemed to him an absurdity, as did also the investing of ideologies and political causes with pseudo-transcendental commitments. In a manner reminiscent of the seventeenth-century French philosopher Blaise Pascal, Butterfield once wrote: "When I reflect on my perversities of pen and tongue, I come to the conclusion that they occur because I am really addressing God to show that I have caught on to His sense of humour—i.e. I am not really anxious enough about the results to be produced in the world of affairs."[6] This was no commonplace flippancy; it was rather the confession of a man who never took himself too seriously, and who in true Augustinian fashion never could conceive of the City of Man, its tragedy and its aspirations in anything but relative terms. One is also led to wonder whether it was in a moment of Christian "perversity" rather than total seriousness that Butterfield in the late 1950s suggested that the West might consider unilaterally ridding itself of nuclear weapons.

In Butterfield's life, Christianity was the source of a lively sense of humor, as well as of that searing skepticism and political detachment summed up in his conclusion to *Christianity and History*: "Hold to Christ, and for the rest be totally uncommitted." Dr. Owen Chadwick, a friend of Butterfield and his successor as Regius Professor of Modern History, has left a memorable portrait of the historian's rare qualities of character and mind:

> He could never be a man of party. The mind was so fresh, so incapable of saying anything second-hand, that he cut across all parties with a dissolving scepticism.
>
> The directness of soul was very important in his influence because his intellectual processes were subtle and agile, at times complex and sinuous. This was a great teacher who liked to disturb every kind of conventional axiom.
>
> . . . he liked to disturb, even to shock; though never crudely nor as with a bludgeon. He used paradox as a way to upset conventional opinion but the paradoxes were always delicate, probing. A friend once came out of a meeting saying, "I can't bear it. Butterfield has been arguing that Machiavelli was a great Christian thinker." He never evaded difficulty; he wrestled, poked around, attempted metaphor, but he never tried to make things easier than they are. . . . You would say that he had a dancing mind, if that epithet did not suggest lack of engagement; a mind able to illuminate with shafts of light and epigrams of wit and flashes of poetry; a man battling with weighty ideas but never heavily, never in burdensome language, never stuffing the brain of his reader with an excess of sawdust. No one ever so used dazzling light to show how anfractuous were the apparently level surfaces of the past.[7]

It was with great reluctance that, during the 1940s, Butterfield began to make public statements on Christianity and to relate his faith to his work as a historian and to the issues of international politics. He was a man of tremendous integrity and he knew well the tendency of our words to outrun our character, the temptation to speak as a Christian in substitution for being one. In 1933 he wrote in his diary of the dangers of parading one's faith in public and observed that "a Christian should talk little of his religion lest he fall into this sin. It is the part of a spiritual man to be austere with his thoughts and to know what is fitting."[8] Largely for this reason, and because of his concern to eschew any form of self-righteousness, he gave up, around 1936, the lay preaching which he had been doing around Cambridge since his days as an undergraduate. Butterfield understood that the foundations of Christian faith had to be inward and its purpose the transformation of one's character, before any authentic public witness could become possible. As he put it in that same 1933 diary entry, "the best evidence of Christianity in the heart is quiet assurance, and a flame that burns in silence, and a charity for ever expressing itself, for ever unexpressed; and with these a serene orderliness and a calm reliance on providence."[9] Only later, when World War II broke out, revealing the full extent of the continuing moral and spiritual crisis of Western civilization, did Butterfield begin offering historical and political commentaries with a distinctly Christian orientation.

As master of Peterhouse (1955–1968) and vice-chancellor of Cambridge from 1959 to 1961 (this was the highest position of leadership in the university, the chancellorship being chiefly an honorary post occupied by men such as the Duke of Edinburgh), Butterfield fought tenacious battles on behalf of the principles of college autonomy and the University's freedom from governmental regulation. Yet he stood out for his rare ability to separate principles from personalities, refusing to make personal enemies of those who opposed him and always mindful that they, too, deserved the respect and tolerance that he thought should be accorded to every human being.

In 1968, after occupying for three years the Regius Professorship of Modern History (the same chair which Lord Acton had held from 1895 to 1902), Butterfield retired to the tranquil village of Sawston, in the hope of completing the history of historiography and what would have been the definitive biography of Charles James Fox. His travels and lecturing and his continuing involvement with the British Committee on the Theory of International Politics were among the endeavors that explain why, upon his death on July 13, 1979, these two major projects remained unfinished.

Ironically enough, however, any study of Butterfield's contribution to the philosophy of international politics must begin with his history of historiography. A survey of the historical mind throughout different cultures and time periods, the attempt, in Acton's celebrated phrase, "to get behind the historian" and discover the hidden philosophical assumptions guiding his methods and results, would yield rich insights into man's views of the processes of time, and thus indirectly into man's perceptions of political reality.[10] Although the discovery of these hidden assumptions was not Butterfield's main impetus for researching the history of history, it was one of its results. The history of history, like Butterfield's wider explorations of the historian's mind and his efforts to relate historical analysis to political prescription, underlined the degree to which historians could make a contribution to the study of international politics supplementing that of the political theorists.

II

The Wisdom of History

History without Politics descends to mere Literature.

John Robert Seeley

2

The origins of history

For Sir Herbert Butterfield, the origins of history and its
subsequent development through the ages was a profound philosophical issue
of great importance to students of politics, religion, and philosophy. The
history of history was likely to shed light on the evolution of human consciousness and on the varied ways in which man interpreted his past and contemporary experiences according to the symbols of his religious world and
the texture of his economic, social, and political conditions. Far from being a
narrow, academic subject of interest only to a few historians, the history of
historiography should be of concern to anyone probing man's endless quest to
understand himself and the world around him. "The story of the development of man's consciousness of history involves a large-scale aspect of the
whole evolution of his experience. It is a major part of his attempt to adjust
himself to the world in which his life is set." From the earliest times to the
present, the writing of history has been connected with man's efforts to derive meaning out of the chaos of his present circumstances and wisdom from
the mistakes and accomplishments of the past. Even in the most primitive
stages of human society, "for the carrying on of life itself, men had to make
terms with history as they understood it. They had to have views about the
way in which things happen, notions about the causes of disasters, ideas
about the character of human destiny, theories about the ups-and-downs of
states." [1]

Not all civilizations, however, have been equally preoccupied with history. Whereas China and the West developed to an advanced degree the science of historiography, the rich civilization of ancient India remained largely
oblivious to it. Some religions and philosophies, such as Hinduism, Bud-
dhism, and Neoplatonism seemed to deny the significance of, and discourage
any interest in, history. Butterfield observed that cultures "soaked in historical
memories" differed considerably in general mentality and in intellectual habits from those which attributed little importance to the study of the past.

Such differences, in turn, affected the development of political thought and of ideas about the nature of international relations.

Western civilization traced its concern with history to the ancient cultures of what today is known as the Middle East. Man's awareness of the past dawned gradually, over the course of many centuries:

> Human beings would be aware of the cycle of the seasons, but also of the way in which the years accumulated, the way they themselves grew older and palaces or temples would fall into ruins. They would be sensible of time's terrible insecurities, of the cataclysm that so often lurked at every fresh turn of the road. They would know the inexorability of death. Their dim reflections on all these things would show themselves, not in specifically historical ideas at first—not in any realm of specialised or technical thought—but in the beliefs and practices of their religion. The emergence of a feeling for history and a sense of the past could come only as part of the development of the whole human outlook. [2]

As human beings grappled with the problem of their destiny, their ensuing religious reflections led them to search for clues in past and contemporary events that would confirm further their religious intuition about the meaning of human existence and the shape of the future. Thus, in the cultures of ancient Mesopotamia and Israel, as in Europe during the Middle Ages, religion and history were intimately connected. Out of religion evolved a series of notions about the course and higher purposes of mundane human events which properly could be called philosophy of history. These philosophical musings sometimes led to the study of the intricacies and technicalities of the events themselves, so that questions of ultimate meaning led to the much narrower ones posed by historical research. Although the notion of history for history's sake failed to take root in the highly religious societies of the ancient Middle East, there were times when a chronicler momentarily would forget his preoccupation with discerning the hand of God in a particular event and become fascinated with the purely mundane questions of how a certain king succeeded in outmaneuvering his powerful adversaries in diplomacy or how a series of economic crises and natural disasters crippled a state's foreign policy. The growth of history was thus simultaneously encouraged by man's religious probings into the meaning of his existence and by curiosity about the workings of specific human events and the actions and decisions of particular human beings. Without either of these forces at work, the study of history might have made an even slower progress than it did.

Stories about a great hero or an extraordinary event, transmitted orally from generation to generation, were perhaps the earliest form of history known to man. These stories sometimes would be joined together into an epic poem, such as the *Iliad*, which would come to represent the history of a people. But, perhaps because of the deep emotional satisfaction it gave its readers, the epic did not always encourage a critical analysis or reappraisal of the past. Another primitive form of history was the lists and records kept by monarchs to enumerate the events of their reign, often with an eye to emphasizing their personal valor, wisdom, and piety towards the gods. One of the oldest of these, the Sumerian King-List, dating back to the year 2000 B.C. or before, records the various changes that took place over the course of centuries as different city-states acquired and lost their predominance over the state-system then existing in southern Mesopotamia. A major impetus to the writing of history, however crude its form, was the endless disputes and wars among states and their rulers. From "the very beginning down to the twentieth century, war has been a more powerful stimulus to historical writing, and a more powerful factor in awaking historical interest than almost anything else." Treaties affixing territorial boundaries or the nature of a state's economic, political, and military relationship to another would be carefully inscribed. They were usually accompanied by a recitation of the political and military events that had led to the agreement and by awe-inspiring accounts of the way in which the gods had rewarded a particular people's righteousness by favoring them in their dealings with neighboring states.[3]

The culture of ancient Mesopotamia, which took root during the third millennium B.C. in the valley formed by the Euphrates and Tigris rivers, produced the first known attempts at a comprehensive interpretation of history. The unpredictability of these rivers and the floods and other natural disasters that regularly plagued the region seemed to point to the vulnerability of life and the discontinuous and cataclysmic nature of history. Notions of divine judgment and punishment for sin were blended into history, as men sought to explain the chaos and evil surrounding them. Scholars have even identified among the literature of the period what seems like a precursor to the Book of Job. Much more than the Egyptians, whose life was infused with order and regularity by the predictable and beneficent behavior of the Nile, the Sumerians were forced to reflect on the broken character of their existence and inquire into the meaning of history. As might be expected, monarchs were not above appropriating and refashioning such interpretations of history for propaganda purposes in the struggle against enemy states. Babylonian kings employed priests to chronicle the rise to greatness of their city, which they attributed to the special affection the god Marduk felt for Babylon over other city-states. Butterfield pointed out, however, that over the long run the entrusting of history writing to priests proved beneficial to the development of historiography. Gradually the priests began to write history less for the sake of national-political purposes, and more out of their philosophical and religious concerns. In time they came to inject into their writings what Butterfield called "the ethical factor in history," the idea that history is not a tale of the simple success of might over right, but a drama in which right is ultimately rewarded and wrong ultimately punished, notwithstanding outward appearances.[4]

The many centuries from 2000 B.C. to the earliest Old Testament documents witnessed further advancement in historiography in the great empires of the Egyptians and the Hittites. As in previous times, the writing of history under kingly patronage reflected the need to impress foreign adversaries with the extent and irreversibility of one's power and to rally one's people to further economic sacrifices on behalf of national glory. Equally significant was the anxiety felt by kings over the judgment future generations might pass on their work, "a dreadful fear" of being unappreciated or, worse yet, forgotten. History writing in the form of dynastic annals or commemorative tablets was thus part of the attempt to control or influence the policies of the state beyond one's brief life span.

Although he devoted considerable attention to the Egyptians, Butterfield was more fascinated with the lesser-known Hittites, partly because of the moral reasonableness and political wisdom he detected in their statecraft and historiography. The annals of the famous Hittite ruler Murshilish amply exhibit some of the qualities proper to good history. The monarch calmly discussed policy choices available to him, showing why he adopted some over others; he did not impute his enemies' behavior to evil, but to political or military circumstances, such as his own weakness, which tempted them to turn against him; and he supported his explanations by reference to speeches, documents, and other bits of historical evidence, rather than to some secret divine knowledge. Butterfield writes that Hittite historiography was affected "by the fact that the monarch is not by any means a solitary tyrant, but more like an overlord, limited by institutions and needing the support of some sort of public opinion"; hence, the constant need to explain actions and policies and the detailed references to past and present historical events. There is none of "the boasting which fills up so much of the space in the Egyptian and Assyrian equivalents. Failures are confessed. And not merely the campaigns of the monarchs but those also of princes and generals are described."[5]

Hittite diplomacy, the political angles of which were of great interest to Butterfield, also made an important contribution to historiography:

> The treaties of the Hittites—and particularly those with vassal-states—differ from all the others of the time that are known to us in that they are preceded by a very considerable historical preamble. These were not perfunctory in character, and it has been noted that, when a renewed conflict led to a further treaty, the old

historical summary was not mechanically taken over as the basis of the new preamble, but a fresh narrative was produced. Also, the other party to the treaty seems to have been allowed to insert his own version of the history in his own copy of the document. In other words, he was not forced to subscribe to what his successful enemy chose to regard as the story of the origin of the trouble— not compelled (somebody has said) to sign a war-guilt clause, like the one imposed on Germany after the end of the First World War.[6]

Butterfield obviously perceived a connection between the reasonableness and moderation of Hittite foreign and domestic policy and the advancement of history in their culture. The search for order and wisdom out of the seemingly chaotic events of the recent past and present was perhaps encouraged by a society aware of the finitude of its power and conscious of the need to found its political arrangements on legitimacy and moral persuasiveness.

Among ancient peoples, the Hebrews' contribution to the development of history was the most original. Here was "a people not only supremely conscious of the past but possibly more obsessed with history than any other nation that has ever existed."[7] The memory of the Exodus forged together numerous disparate tribes into the nation of Israel, giving to that nation an identity that to this day has resisted successfully the disintegrating impact of thousands of years. It was firm adherence to a common historical heritage, more than any unities of geography, language, or political systems, that held the ancient Hebrews together.

Unlike most of the great civilizations surrounding them, the Hebrews believed that history had an ultimate purpose towards which it was inevitably moving. The future would witness the fulfillment of God's promise to his people, the arrival of a great new era. In contrast to the cyclic view of history held by the Greeks and Hindus, the Hebrews' conception "provided a framework within which an idea of progress could develop" later in the course of Western civilization.[8] Although the Hebrews were not the first to wrestle with the problems of evil and suffering in history, they were original in putting forth the idea that earthly misfortunes are not only an expression of God's judgment on human sin, but also can be an indication of His special favor. Those whom the Lord loves, He chastises. Through their sufferings, the chosen people were purified and prepared to carry out their mission of bringing all the other nations of the earth to Yahweh. This biblical idea had at least three important implications. First, this was the earliest known appearance of the concept of the "historic mission" of a nation, which would play such a large role in European political history. Second, the simpler notion that God showers earthly prosperity upon the righteous was overshadowed by the profound recognition that to be chosen by God could mean to be chosen to suffer; that is the locus of the Christian idea, which has exerted a powerful influence in Western civilization, that suffering and brokenness need not be feared, for they reveal man's true insufficiency before God, propelling him to charity towards his neighbors. Third, the disappointments and tragic denouements with which human existence is replete were not part of an all-embracing chaos and meaningless pervading history. Instead, they were, or could be, transformed into instruments of the higher redemptive purposes of God in human affairs. Man could live in the midst of suffering and evil because, in ways unknown to us, these may "have their place in a higher economy of Providence."[9] Man's sin and foibles must lead him to repentance, but not despair; for, out of the havoc man wreaks upon the world, the divine mercy can bring greater good than that which man initially destroyed. This philosophically problematical conception, which should not be confused with Panglossian assertions that this is the best of all possible worlds, helped historians from St. Augustine down to Leopold von Ranke and Butterfield to affirm the possibility of political renewal, hope, and even temporary improvement in an undeniably catastrophic world.

The key concepts that characterized the religion of ancient Israel, those of the promise, the covenant, the judgment, and the mission, were formulated on the basis of specific historical events. The nation's legal foundations, the Ten Commandments, were not grounded so much on philosophical or ethical reasoning as on history: the Lord rescued his people from the bondage of Egypt and gave them the law, which Israel should obey in faithfulness and gratitude to the One who saved her and established her as a nation. Moreover, by connecting the Hebrews' historical roots with the origins of mankind in the book of Genesis, the Old Testament encouraged reflection on the history of all nations. Until the middle of the eighteenth century, almost every universal history produced by European civilization began with Genesis.

With the exception of the first book of Maccabees, which Butterfield considered among "the best that ever came down to us from the ancient world," the last few centuries of Jewish history prior to the birth of Christ were largely sterile in historical acumen.[10] Butterfield attributed this in part to the weakening of a rich tension underlying earlier Hebrew historical writings. In the Old Testament, two complementary perspectives on the action of God in history existed side by side. The better-known one emphasized direct divine intervention in everyday human affairs, such as the crossing of the Red Sea, and pointed to a correlation between human sin and the divine judgment as expressed by particular natural or political disasters. Another, subtly interwoven in various texts, reminded man that God often acts in history, not by interfering directly with the processes of nature or politics but by working in every person's heart, and that the rewards of the righteous may lie in an inner closeness to God and a joy that transcend this world. This second perspective, found in the Wisdom literature for instance, indirectly encouraged curiosity about the workings of history and politics because it posited the existence of a sphere of human action which, while remaining under God's care, was not subject to continuous, detailed divine interference; some aspects of human experience, where there seemed to be considerable scope for human freedom and creativity, could be studied with the due attention to causal relationships and objective circumstances that is so important to good historiography. Because man does not know fully God's ways and because God allows in the world patterns of order whereby there is "a time to weep, and a time to laugh, a time to mourn, and a time to dance," a defeat in war need not be explained wholly as divine judgment but also could be described with reference to the ordinary human actions that led to it.

After the exile and return from Babylonian captivity, this tension between the transcendent and the secular, which never had been anything better than precarious, began to give way to a religious-political Messianism which claimed that "not by the actions of men or by the ordinary processes of history, but by the direct action of God in the fullness of time, the terrestrial glories of the Davidic Kingdom would be established." To use Eric Voegelin's language, the transcendent future envisioned by the prophets was immanentized. With notable exceptions, the remembrance of God's mighty deeds in the past was overshadowed by efforts to refine the law so as to avoid another future judgment and by an apocalyptic literature "which presented a new heaven and a new earth, visions of celestial powers, a realm that was like a mythology highly transcendentalised." It was "a flight from history."[11] From Butterfield's viewpoint, the tension between the transcendent and the secular was at the core of good historiography and, as he had argued in other writings, at the core of good political theory and practical ethics as well.

The Greeks did not have a historical memory comparable to that of the Hebrews in either length of time or thematic grandeur. They also were saddled with a cyclic view of time that denied to history any ultimate purpose. Nevertheless, their scientific curiosity and the high regard they had for the political independence of their city-states helped them to achieve for the first time a truly scientific historiography whose insight and understanding many consider unsurpassed. Hippocrates discussed, with detailed inquisitiveness, the negative impact that geography, climate, and conditions of political despotism can have on a people's ability to wage war. In a world previously accustomed to thinking that events came from the arbitrary wills of men and gods, it was of great significance to read a disquisition in which human behavior was explained by reference to the influences of climate and political institutions. The fifth century B.C. was to the Greeks what the twentieth has been to our modern civilization, a time of intense international conflict and unremitting political struggle. The rising of the Ionian cities against the Persians, Xerxes' invasion of Greece and his subsequent defeat, and the tragic Peloponnesian war among the Greek city-states stimulated Hecateus, Herodotus, and Thucydides to produce their incomparable masterpieces of historical analysis and writing. As has often been the case, the great cataclysms of international politics prodded human beings to the study of history and man's political behavior in it. A peculiar feature of the great historical works of the Greeks was that they "assume the existence of political consciousness in their readers." As Butterfield explains:

> The birth of Greek historiography is connected with the rise of the Greek city-state and the establishment of a broadly based government inside the various cities. . . . Men felt that their own lives and interests were tied up with the fate of their city and of the Greek people; and it is significant that Hippocrates should have made so much of this point in making the comparison with the people of Asia. The fortunes of one's state became a major preoccupation, therefore, and the place occupied by one's city in the given region and the given time—the city viewed as the historian would view it—was a principal conditioning factor in one's life. Where men are citizens and not merely subjects, their political consciousness carries with it also a consciousness of history—on the one hand a realisation that they are living in history, creatures of time and circumstance, and on the other hand a feeling that the past of the body politic is really their own past.[12]

Because it had grown independently from the sources of Western civilization, Chinese historiography was of special interest to Butterfield. From its earliest stages, Chinese history paid close attention to natural phenomena such as floods, earthquakes, droughts, and planetary movements, which it regarded as important as the actions of human beings. Historical writing in China "was affected by the view that an intrinsic relationship or a special sympathy exists between the workings of nature and the workings of history."[13] This was a contrast to Western historiography, which, especially after the rise of Christianity, made a sharp distinction between history and nature, history being essentially the interplay of human relations and nature merely the backdrop or stage for this drama.[14]

A combination of special circumstances made China a history-conscious culture. The ancient teaching that "virtue was to be achieved only by following the example of one's ancestors" provided a strong incentive to the study of the past. The famous manual for rulers, the *Shoo King*, blended counsels of political morality with urgings such as "study antiquity as you enter upon your office" and "employ the men of old families in the work of government." Whereas in Greece philosophy had been indifferent to history, if not antihistorical, in China it had the opposite effect.[15] Chinese philosophy "drove men to the consideration of the concrete world, and made them seize on tangible facts, demonstrable situations." Its method of argument was not the establishment of logical links between abstract concepts derived from inner contemplation but rather "a persuasive power, depending on rhetorical devices." A favorite, if not the most effective, rhetorical device was "the exploitation, in one way or another, of historical examples. There was a party to be persuaded, a prince to be won over. The object might not be attainable by an austere chain of deductive reasoning. It was more to the point if one could make apt allusions to great men" of former ages. Moreover, China did not have as vast a repository of myth as the Greeks had, and for many centuries it stood isolated from other countries and civilizations. Chinese thinkers reflecting on the current state of politics and culture in their land had no point of perspective, no source of comparison, other than the one they could find by studying or speculating on their nation's own past.[16]

By making a return to the wisdom of the past the centerpiece of their ethical and political theory, Confucius and his disciples further strengthened the position of history in Chinese culture. Also, through their work, Chinese historiography became much more moralizing, without losing its basically secular character. Confucian philosophy asserted the reality of a moral judgment throughout history which rewarded the state and its leaders according to their virtues and vices. But the heaven issuing this judgment was an impersonal, cosmic process, reflecting nothing more than the way in which the universe happened to be constituted. "It was not through arbitrary interventions of gods, whose sense of right had been outraged, but by . . . the processes of history itself, that the wicked met their punishment" and unvirtuous states declined. There was an awareness that the descent from political virtue into vice was not always the work of a few evildoers but the consequence of that curiously obverse relationship between vice and virtue: all too easily, courage becomes transformed into militarism, fairness into permissiveness, industriousness into greed. Some Chinese historians sensed that in the political world the fall from virtue could come about through the imbalances which virtue itself could create.[17] For twentieth-century Americans the story seems familiar. The compassion underlying the welfare state, when carried too far, led to a society in which thrift and self-initiative are punished. The noble sense of mission born out of World War II led to an arrogance of power and the Vietnam debacle. Lord Acton's profound ethical insight, "when you perceive a truth, look for a balancing truth," seemed to be adumbrated in Chinese historiography, and it permeated much of Butterfield's thinking as well.[18]

The intimate connection in China between political theory and practice on the one hand and the writing of history on the other was not free of problems. In the year 221 B.C., a new dynasty resolved to strengthen its authority by obliterating the moral, political, and historical teachings of traditional Chinese thought, including Confucianism. In an episode reminiscent of Mao's cultural revolution of 1966, the Emperor decreed the infamous burning of the books, the wholesale destruction of the classics of Chinese historiography and philosophy. Anyone appealing to antiquity or tradition was subject to the death penalty. This aberration came to an end a few years later when another ruling family, friendly to Confucianism, came to power, spawning a renaissance of historical studies.

The key turning point in the development of historiography in Western civilization was the emergence of Christianity and its subsequent influence. Although the early Christians were more concerned with evangelism than the study of the past, several features of the faith were bound to give its followers a growing historical consciousness as time went on. First, there was the close relationship between the New Testament and the Old Testament, centered around the idea that Jesus Christ had come "in the fullness of time," to carry out that which the prophets had foretold. As Butterfield explains, the exposition of that relationship was likely "to produce interesting ideas about the march of history, the processes of time, the way in which the past prepares for the future." Time acquired purpose. It played "a part in human destiny and became a generative factor. . . . What came earlier must by necessity have been imperfect, and time was needed for its completion." Here was another seed of the modern idea of progress.[19]

Second, the great affirmations of Christianity, the Incarnation, the Crucifixion, and the Resurrection, were inextricably connected with history and were proclaimed as factual events that had taken place in the midst of the secular world. Even St. John's Gospel, often considered the most mystical of the four gospels, emphasized that "the Word was made flesh, and dwelt among us, and we beheld his glory . . . full of grace and truth." The New Testament was replete with similar assertions concerning the historicity of these events and the existence of numerous witnesses to them. As decades and centuries passed, the Church, eager to preserve faithfully the teachings of Jesus and the disciples, nurtured its historical consciousness further. Arguments over the validity of theological doctrines or the hierarchy of authority were carried out by appeals to history, by references to the original sources of the faith.

Not until the Christians became fully integrated into Rome's social and political order, however, did they develop any comprehensive philosophies of history. The first major effort in this direction was undertaken by Eusebius, who lived during the reign and conversion to Christianity of the Emperor Constantine. From Butterfield's perspective, Eusebius offered too crude a correlation between the hand of Providence and the everyday affairs of the world, between God's judgment and the course of politics. Overlooking the paradox of wicked emperors who lived to ripe old age, Eusebius ascribed Constantine's long life and his dazzling triumphs in foreign and domestic policy to his conversion. History was reaching its climax now that the most powerful empire on earth was a Christian empire. Under God's hand, the few nations remaining outside Rome's orb would be gathered in and a long era of world peace and unity would begin. Eusebius' association of the divine will with earthly political grandeur was "a glorification of sheer success," "a kind of political theology" in which secular history became sacred.[20]

A much more profound Christian interpretation of history was produced by St. Augustine, with whom Butterfield felt a special kinship, being indebted to him for much of his own thought on the relations among Christianity, history, and politics. Living a century after Eusebius, Augustine knew the evils that could exist even when Rome was under Christian rulers; in his lifetime he witnessed Rome's sack by the Vandals and the empire's rapid disintegration. Consequently, he grappled with the problem of God's judgments in history differently. He pointed out that God sent the sunshine and the rain on the just and unjust alike; this was also true of military and political success. If there was a difference between the Christians and the pagans, it was that the Christians need not curse suffering and despair over it but see it as something which could refine their character and correct their imperfections.

While God's Providence did not always reward Christian virtue with worldly success, it often did reward worldly virtue with worldly success. The Roman Republic had flourished thanks to the worldly virtue of those pagans who had been willing to sacrifice their lives and private fortunes for the good of the state. Even the Romans of the late republic and early empire received, in the form of Pax Romana, the reward for their courage and love of glory; their virtues were superior to the love of ease and pleasure which eventually infected Rome, leading to the debacles of Augustine's day. The noble pagans of ancient Rome were, in Augustine's words, "good in their own way"; they were "laudable doubtless and glorious according to human judgment." In their discipline and faithfulness to the earthly city, they could serve as examples to the members of the heavenly city. "Verily, they have their reward," said Augustine, quoting the Scriptures.[21]

Augustine thus granted to the realm of political history a degree of autonomy which Butterfield prized. The earthly city, though not outside the sovereignty of God, is allowed considerable freedom of political ends and means, some of them relatively better than others but all of them geared to serve the earthly city's worldly purposes. God does not routinely intervene in the ceaseless conflicts among the world's kingdoms. He indiscriminately allows to men and nations the joys of victory and sorrows of destruction, which are the fruits of the relentless pursuit of glory, power, and material goods into which men plunge themselves. The Augustinian separation of the City of God from the City of Man served a Christian historian such as Butterfield well. He was free to engage in the dispassionate study of history without the need to discover who were the good and the wicked, without the need to make absolute moral judgments on matters which after all were suitable only for relative evaluations. Moreover, the City of Man had its own wisdom and virtue which, though insufficient to make men wise unto eternal salvation, had their proper place in the scheme of divine Providence. Therefore, a Christian historian could study the intricate workings of politics, the detailed rules of the grammar of power, and speculate on the ways in which a semblance of temporary order and civility might be brought to the restless course of international politics.

The development of historical criticism in modern Europe formed another important chapter in the history of historiography. One of the earliest landmarks was the demonstration in 1440 by the humanist Laurentius Valla of the spurious character of the Donation of Constantine, a document in which the Emperor allegedly conveyed the western half of the Roman Empire to the pope. Of similar importance was the work of La Popelinière, who, by the use of rigorous historical criticism, disproved in 1599 the popular belief that the ancestors of the French, the Franks, were direct descendants of the Trojans. A major spur to the development of historical criticism was the bitter controversies between Protestants and Catholics during the sixteenth and seventeenth centuries over issues of ecclesiastical and political history. As each side sought to discredit the other's historical interpretations and strengthen its own case, both were forced to refine the techniques of historical criticism. As the eighteenth century moved on, the methods of historical criticism began to be applied even to the Bible, the most famous of these early biblical critics being Jean Astruc, who sought to prove that Moses had written parts of the Pentateuch from sources dated prior to his lifetime.

Butterfield agreed with Lord Acton, however, that the modern era of historical criticism really began in 1824, with the publication of Leopold von Ranke's *Zur Kritik neuer Geschichtschreiber (Criticism of Modern Historical Writing)*. In "a great reversal of the assumption on which historical writing had been based from the earliest civilisations," Ranke argued that scholars studying Renaissance Italy could not simply rely on the accounts written by historians living in that period, such as Guicciardini. They had to go to the very documentary sources on which those historians supposedly had based their contemporary histories: government documents, public and private correspondence, etc. Eventually, notes Butterfield, Ranke realized that the exacting canons of historical criticism had to be applied even to these original sources. Historians sifting through the famed dispatches of seventeenth century Venetian ambassadors could not take these reports at face value. They had to put themselves in the place of the ambassadors, and they needed a sound understanding of the workings of foreign policy in order to ask themselves what role an ambassador's personal characteristics and the goals and ambitions of his state might have played in inclining a dispatch towards a particular viewpoint.[22]

In the hands of Ranke, diplomatic history thus became closely linked with political theory and a series of beliefs on the nature of man and the behavior of states in international politics. For all its technical proficiency, historical criticism risked failing to place the multitudinous events of international politics within the larger framework of which they were a part, unless the historian kept in mind the larger issues of human nature and the patterns of international political behavior displayed by man in previous ages. In other words, the historian of international relations needed an understanding of political theory and international politics. During the course of the twentieth century, one branch of this evolving tradition of diplomatic history which Ranke influenced so heavily replaced his philosophical idealism with a political realism that, as in Butterfield's case, was in part the fruit of two catastrophic world wars.

In spite of their strenuous defense of "technical history," of historical criticism for its own sake, neither Ranke nor Butterfield thought that history could be totally separated from political philosophy. Lord Acton accused Ranke of the contrary when he wrote that

> history, in Ranke's conception, is a science complete in itself, independent, and ancillary to none, borrowing no instruments, and supplying no instruction, beyond its own domain. This dignified isolation involves a certain poverty in the reflections, a certain inadequacy of generalization. The writer seldom illustrates his facts from the state of ancient or general learning, or by the investigation of the legal and constitutional problems. He does not explain the phenomena by political laws, the teaching of observation and comparison; and he has no care for literature, or for the things, apart from politics which manifest the life and thought of nations.[23]

Anyone who reads Ranke's classic essay, "The Great Powers," or his *Universal History*, written toward the end of his life, is forced to revise Acton's appraisal. The same could be said of Butterfield's writings. Despite some of the things he wrote in *The Whig Interpretation of History* and elsewhere about the need to recognize the autonomy of technical history, he did not think that the historian could remain content with the verification and recitation of facts. True, as he liked to say, all the facts associated with the Reformation were capable of being established and accepted regardless of whether one was a Protestant or a Catholic. But when the time came, as it always must for any great mind, to reflect on the implications of the Reformation for man's political and religious life then and today, these were questions the answers to which involved recourse to one's theology and political philosophy. To overlook the distinction between technical history and philosophy of history was no worse than to reduce the historian's work to the pure research of facts.

Perhaps the difference between Acton on the one hand and Ranke and Butterfield on the other was not that the latter tried to develop a "value-free" history, but that they simply tried to give technical history as much scope as it properly deserved and put off for as long as possible the time when it was necessary to take off the fact finder's hat and put on the philosopher's. Butterfield, of course, did not think that the historian's philosophy, politics, or religion had a higher authority than those of the philosopher or political theorist simply because it proceeded out of a historian's mind. In this respect, therefore, he underlined technical research as the task for which the historian was best equipped by his tools; the ascertainment of facts was the historian's chief business. Yet, neither Butterfield nor Ranke discouraged the historian, once he had done his work, from drawing on the facts to embark on the kind of creative interpretive enterprise essential to a reflective human existence. Butterfield would not have objected, that is, so long as the historian did not try to give to his political or theological interpretations the kind of scientific validity fit only for the ascertainment of facts.

In the history of historiography, the development of historical criticism coincided with what Butterfield called "the great secularisation," the gradual decline of the leadership which the Christian world view enjoyed for more than a thousand years over the writing of history in the West. It was not that Butterfield thought there was a clear-cut adverse relationship between a society's depth of religious conviction and its ability to produce good historiography; after all, "the pious man can have a clear eye for the world of concrete things, and can have his feet close to earth, without losing his spiritual outlook." Butterfield sometimes "wondered whether Christianity does not give men a clearer vision of the facts and the factual setting than the pagan beliefs of either the past or the present often have." Perhaps, as he put it, "only through Christianity can one acquire a healthy kind of worldly-mindedness."[24] The Hittites' belief that the gods issued their moral judgments in the course of history did not prevent them from offering sophisticated, purely secular explanations for various events. And faith in a transcendent God did not keep the author of the Book of Maccabees or Augustine in the *City of God* from achieving penetrating insights into the political and military affairs of their time that rivaled those of contemporary pagan historians. The problem came, as in the case of Eusebius, when one tried to impose the patterns of the City of God on the rather different ways of the City of Man, when the religious historian interpreted a particular event as the action of God and stopped inquiring into the earthly processes by which that event had come about. But such a failing was not the sole property of Christians; the devotees of progress, reason, science, or the victory of the proletariat failed as easily whenever they tried to fit the rich and tempestuous course of human history into their particular teleology.

Historiography, by virtue of its purpose of drawing our minds to the study of political and other earthly events had, according to Butterfield, a built-in tendency to concern itself with the secular. Yet, curiously enough, from time immemorial to the present, men repeatedly pointed to Providence, the hand of God, or any number of nonreligious equivalents to help explain that which seemed unexplainable in the course of history. For instance, the predominantly secular historical thought of the Renaissance, as that of ancient Greece, ascribed a decisive importance to what Machiavelli and others called fortune. There was an irreducible, unexplainable element of chance and contingency which played a critical role in human affairs; in Butterfield's words, this was "almost like bringing the gods into the story . . . by a back door," in the same way that secular-minded twentieth-century people might substitute the concept of luck for that of divine favor.[25] During the eighteenth and nineteenth centuries, "lapsed Christians" such as Voltaire, Herder, and Hegel produced impressive secular philosophies of history in which reason and progress played the role formerly reserved to God's hand. It was these grandiose philosophies of history that Leopold von Ranke opposed. Whereas the Enlightenment philosophers and their nineteenth century heirs "thought they could use history to discover the meaning of life, or, rather, to illustrate their view of the meaning of life," Ranke passionately insisted "that history sets out, using tremendous engines of research, just to discover what actually did happen—what observable things can be demonstrated to have happened."[26]

If many Christian historians have had difficulty in separating the secular from the transcendent in history, the City of Man from the City of God, or the realm of factual history from philosophy of history, Butterfield did not. Indeed, for him Christianity was capable not only of giving the historian or political theorist "a healthy kind of worldly-mindedness," it also provided one with a firm foundation from which to survey dispassionately and accurately the bewildering diversity and unexpected paradoxes of human existence. As he put it at the end of his celebrated *Christianity and History*, "We can do worse than remember a principle which both gives us a firm Rock and leaves us the maximum elasticity for our minds: the principle: Hold to Christ, and for the rest be totally uncommitted."[27]

The Christian historian did not need to fear the directions into which his research might take him, nor did he have to impose any preconceived patterns on the course of history. His attitude should be one of a humble student, ever eager to learn of, and marvel at, the intricate complexities of human affairs, beholding their tumultuous course, not with the anxiety of those eager to vindicate their political causes but with the serenity of those who take seriously God's sovereignty. The Christian historian did not need to hide the barbarities of the religious wars, for they were a sobering reminder of man's universal sin which permeated even the life of the Church; nor did he have to deny the triumphs of secular civilization and science that were a testimony to man's creative power, for these pointed to the Creator's grandeur. This elasticity of mind, this firm refusal to elevate relativities to the level of absolutes, was as characteristic of Butterfield the political thinker as of Butterfield the historian.

Although he worked on it for the last twenty-five years of his life, Butterfield did not complete to his satisfaction his beloved history of historiography. It is not difficult to understand, however, why he ascribed such importance to the endeavor. A subject which might strike many readers as the epitome of arid antiquarianism, the history of history was in his hands a rich mirror reflecting many facets of man's religious and political experience and their evolution throughout different cultures and time periods. An inquiry into what made man curious about his past was one way of discovering the great themes of man's dialogue with himself throughout the ages, those timeless questions which continually have engaged his intellect and heart. An awareness of these questions and of the existential dilemmas to which they pointed was a prerequisite to gaining a better understanding of man and his turbulent political life. "The history of historiography," he said, "comes to points at which it carries us beyond its own domain, and breaks into a realm of profounder questioning."[28]

3

The mind of the historian

Shortly after Butterfield's death in the summer of 1979, one of his colleagues at Peterhouse, Maurice Cowling, wrote a review of his life and work in which he observed that the center of Butterfield's intellectual life "was not professional or 'technical' history, as he chose to call it, but a tension of which he was acutely conscious between historical thinking as a profession and historical thinking as prophecy, religion, or general culture."[1] This was the same tension Butterfield had discerned in the historical writings of the Hittites, the Hebrews, and some of the Christian historians such as Augustine. While the second pole of this tension accounts for Butterfield's rich philosophical interpretations of history, which will be closely examined in the next chapter, the first pole was of equal importance to his thinking and curiously enough had significant implications for his ideas on statecraft and diplomacy.

Butterfield was well aware of the major role played by historians, consciously or unconsciously, in the shaping of political theory and practice. In his interpretation of the facts, the historian was bound to insert his philosophical and political presuppositions sooner or later; the sooner he openly acknowledged these presuppositions and the later he brought them into play the better, but there was no way to avoid the insertion. The close connection between the study of history and the course of politics took place at two different levels. One was the level of interpretation or philosophy of history, the other was that of technical historical research. Concerning the first level he wrote:

> The problems of historiography are at certain points closely connected with the problems of life. They touch the question of the way in which human beings are to take their vicissitudes on the earth—the way in which nations are to reflect on their corporate experience. . . . Over and over again we discover to what a degree, in politics for example, men do their thinking and form

their attitudes by reference to some presumed picture of the pro-
cession of the centuries. The framework which people give to
their general history—the notion they have of man in time and of
the processes of time—may do much to determine the rest of their
outlook. . . . It is possible for historians to mislead a nation in
respect of what it might regard as its historic mission. It is possible for them to give men a wrong notion of what they can do
with their destiny. . . . The nineteenth-century myth of romantic
nationalism would appear to have been born of historical study—
it could hardly have come into existence if men had not been so
interested in delving into the past.[2]

The power of historians over man's political consciousness and behavior
had grown during the nineteenth and twentieth centuries, partly as a result of
the decline of Christianity's intellectual and social influence. Historians became the new prophets and history the new revelation of human destiny. Political ideas nurtured on the historical oversimplifications of Hegel, Marx,
Spengler, and numerous others took hold of the imaginations of millions,
contributing to the disorders of totalitarianism, revolutionary terror, and
total war which continue to afflict Western civilization to this day. A favorite
illustration of the historians' political power was the way in which a group of
nineteenth-century German historians, including von Sybel and Treitschke,
influenced the development of their country's political institutions in the twin
directions of authoritarianism and centralization. According to Butterfield,

the historian . . . played an important part in the German national
story . . . for in effect it was he who said to the country: "See, this
is your tradition, this is the line which the past has set for you to
follow." And now it is dawning on the Germans that their historians may have made the wrong diagnosis. In their function of
eliciting or discerning the essential traditions of their country they
may have led their contemporaries astray. In Bismarck's time one
historian, Gervinus, pointed out that the militarism of Prussia was
only a comparatively recent appendix to the story. It was limited to
a couple of hundred years and superimposed upon a much longer
tradition of federalism, local autonomy, free cities, and lax government. . . . Hamburg would have provided Germany with a
capital more congenial to her essential traditions than Berlin. But
he was dismissed as an historian of small-state psychology, too hostile to the Hohenzollern dynasty. Historians cannot prevent their
work from having an effect in the world; and it seems that they
perform a function which they do not always desire to exercise.
They help to elicit or to diagnose their country's traditions; or

rather, perhaps, as we have seen, they give added leverage or confirmation to the decision which their contemporaries are already making on this point.[3]

Although Butterfield criticized what he called "the Whig interpretation of history" that had dominated much of British historiography, he recognized and appreciated its mark on British political life: "it was to prove of the greatest moment to us that by the early seventeenth century our antiquarians had formulated our history as a history of liberty."[4] Yet he thought that besides "the discovery or the underlining of a tradition there seems to be a sense in which the historian may represent the thoughts of a nation as it reflects on its own triumphs or vicissitudes."[5] Some of the differences in outlook between English and French historical thought, for example, might be explained by the fact that "the English, remembering the seventeenth-century civil wars, decided that revolution was a thing which must not be allowed ever to happen again; while the French, recalling the events of the 1790's, tended rather to idealise revolution."[6] In a similar fashion, the tragic experiences of the German people during the Nazi period and World War II inspired a new generation of German historians in the postwar era to reassess their nation's past and offer a vision of Germany's place in the world different from that of the late nineteenth-century school.[7]

In other words, there was a symbiotic relation between the historian and the political world in which he lived. He could not but influence in one direction or another the course of political ideas, but at the same time his thinking was unavoidably framed within the limitations and terms of his generation's political debates and reflections. The relationship could be of a therapeutic and regenerative kind, as with the postwar German historians, or it could have the highly detrimental effect of strengthening the worst political tendencies of the moment. To this whole dilemma Butterfield offered a partial and tentative solution that was perhaps the best anyone could offer:

> If we can never remove the subjective element from our narratives and expositions, we can neutralize it somewhat by realising how men are conditioned, and seeing that some of the hidden things are brought up into our consciousness. It is something to have a glimpse of the subtle and manifold ways in which a whole miscellany of unexpected conditioning circumstances have helped to mould the historical mind in one period and another. It is through the neglect of this self-discipline that in one age after another history operates to confirm the prevailing fallacies and ratify the favourite errors of the time—even magnifying prejudices at each stage of the story by projecting them back upon the canvas of all the centuries.[8]

One of the merits of the history of historiography was that it could help the student to "get behind the historian" and sift some of the historian's prejudices out of a particular historical interpretation. The issue of the origins of World War I, for example, could be clarified considerably by studying the successive historical interpretations offered to explain it and then putting together one giant collage incorporating the insights that seemed most accurate and leaving out those tainted by the apparent prejudices and limitations of the various historians. Even if in the end there were still questions left largely unanswered, the procedure had the advantage of alerting the student to those points of interpretation on which there seemed to be broad agreement as distinct from those yet unresolved.

While he was aware of the links of philosophy of history to politics, Butterfield also perceived an intimate connection between the methods of historical science and those of good statecraft. The qualities and way of thinking required of a technical historian were in many respects remarkably similar to those essential for a successful diplomat. Thus, it may be no surprise that a man who spent much of his life pondering what it was that made a good historian also produced some of the most profound commentaries on classical diplomacy known in the twentieth century. Like the technical historian, a diplomat needed a creative imagination and the capacity to put himself in the place of those with whom he was negotiating. A good diplomat should see the world not only from his country's standpoint but also from that of other states. The work of both the historian and the diplomat was more likely to be attuned to the reality of the human condition if they surveyed the vast map of international politics, not with an eye to distinguishing the good from the wicked but with a sense of man's "universal sinfulness," with an awareness that every state, including one's own, had a share of responsibility for those tragic deadlocks of fear and national pride at the root of international conflict. Equally important was that elusive quality Butterfield called "elasticity of mind." It encompassed a general reluctance to elevate relatives to absolutes or to see the course of events as predetermined in one direction. For the diplomat it also implied what Hans Morgenthau, a friend of Butterfield, described as the ability to distinguish secondary issues from vital issues. Elasticity of mind also meant that the diplomat, like the historian, needed to see the map of political forces, not as frozen or unchangeable but as ever fluid and evolving, with imperceptible shifts and transformations gradually taking place under the seemingly rigid surface, suddenly bringing about open ruptures and realignments in political relationships, which the diplomat had to be ready to exploit boldly and creatively.

With a characteristic penchant for analogies, Butterfield compared the imaginative historian to a Sherlock Holmes:

At the first stage you have the stupid inspector from Scotland Yard who sees all the obvious clues, falls into all the traps, makes all the commonsense inferences, and lo! the criminal is self-evident. The whole story of the crime in fact is immediately made clear to us; there is a plausible role in that story for each of the characters concerned; the solution satisfies the mind, or at any rate the mind at a given level. . . . Detective stories may not in other ways be true to life, but it is the case in human affairs that the same set of clues, envisaged at a higher level of thought, with or without additional evidence—the same set of clues reshaped into a new synthesis by a Sherlock Holmes—may produce a new map of the whole affair, an utterly unexpected story to narrate, and possibly even a criminal where in the first place we had never thought to look for one.[9]

This capacity for a comprehensive interpretation of human events and personalities, for "a new synthesis" of understanding that went beyond commonplace observations and prejudices, was essential to the diplomat as well.

Throughout his life, therefore, Butterfield was intimately concerned with the historian's mind, with the way history is conceived and written. His first work was *The Historical Novel*, published when he was a youthful twenty-four. It was a study of the role which the literary imagination can play in the reconstruction of past historical events. The historian, he argued, had to cultivate the skills of the imagination, often reserved only for novelists and poets, in order to capture something of the ways of thinking and feeling of human beings culturally and chronologically far removed from him. In a review of Butterfield's historical corpus fifty years later, a critic was to remark that "no one ever saw more clearly than Butterfield the part which the imagination or intuition plays in the apprehension of the past."[10]

The themes adumbrated in *The Historical Novel* bore ample fruit a few years later in *The Peace Tactics of Napoleon, 1806–1808*, a rich study of the political, diplomatic, and military events surrounding the Peace of Tilsit, which Butterfield undertook with the encouragement of Harold Temperley, then the dean of British diplomatic historians. The book combined meticulous research of the vast mass of documentary sources available with the imaginativeness of interpretation and narrative that Butterfield had earlier prescribed to historians. Its masterful treatment of the intricate diplomacy of Napoleon and his adversaries during the critical period between the battle of Jena and the famous summit between Napoleon and Czar Alexander I in a raft on the Niemen River foreshadowed Butterfield's later studies on statecraft, international politics, and diplomacy. His portrayal of Napoleon, Alexander, and the Prussian King Frederick William III won the praise of many critics. It revealed a marked sensitivity to the interactions among the complex personalities of these political leaders and an appreciation of the chaotic circumstances engulfing statesmen over which they do not always have control. Already in this early work, Butterfield had a Thucydidean awareness of the important role played in diplomacy by the personal qualities, the human strengths and shortcomings, of its authors. The warning he issued then was equally relevant to historians, practicing diplomats, and political scientists too enamored of their behavioralist methodologies:

> There is something in the history of diplomacy which inclines to be cold and forbidding, and lacks the full-blooded leap of the larger story of human lives. Like the history of institutions it will tend to concern itself with the development of a system, abstracted from its human context; it will aspire to the mathematical theorem. There is a balancing of forces, and adjustment of interests; there is much that proceeds out of the logic of a situation, there is much that seems to come by a kind of automatic interaction. Sometimes, in rationalisation, one can almost forget that human beings are at work, with play of mind and mood and impulse; acts will not seem to cry out for an explanation in personality, but will be referred to some logic of policy. And history will fall to her greatest temptation—hearing the tick of the clock, but forgetting to feel the pulse.[11]

Butterfield's consuming interest in the nature of historiography achieved a new high point with the publication in 1931 of *The Whig Interpretation of History*, which he dedicated to his former tutor Paul Vellacott, a lifelong Conservative. This now classic essay was a critique of that kind of historiography which tends to see history as a mighty struggle between good and evil, between the forces of liberalism and progress on one hand and those of conservatism and reaction on the other. The Whig historian looked at history from the viewpoint of his own times, and for him historical change seemed a preordained process leading up to the supposed triumph of liberalism and progress in modern times. The three main features of a Whig version of history were the notion of inevitable progress, a penchant for tracing contemporary categories of thought back to alleged remote origins, and the meting out of moral judgments on past historical characters according to their contributions or obstructions to the march of modernity.

The Whig historian did not derive his assumptions on the meaning of history from research on particular historical events. On the contrary, he superimposed his preconceived notions on the research itself. Even when the results of historical research suggested, for example, that the eighteenth-century statesman Charles James Fox was not the pristine apostle of liberty that Whig historians claimed him to be, the Whig historian would fit the outcome of his research within the procrustean bed of his world view. This attitude, wrote Butterfield, "represents a fallacy and an unexamined habit of mind, into which we fall when we treat of history on the broad scale . . . it inserts itself at the change of focus that we make when we pass from the microscopic view of a particular period to our bird's-eye view of the whole." [12] Against the Whig view of history and its accompanying methodology, Butterfield asserted that

> real historical understanding is not achieved by the subordination of the past to the present, but rather by our making the past our present and attempting to see life with the eyes of another century than our own. It is not reached by assuming that our own age is the absolute to which Luther and Calvin and their generation are only relative; it is only reached by fully accepting the fact that their generation was as valid as our generation, their issues as momentous as our issues and their days as full and as vital to them as our day is to us. The twentieth century which has its own hairs to split may have little patience with Arius and Athanasius who burdened the world with a quarrel about a diphthong, but the historian has not achieved historical understanding . . . until he has seen that the diphthong was bound to be the most urgent matter in the universe to those people. [13]

The historian's task was not to condemn or to idolize but to understand, to put himself in the place of past historical figures in such a way that he came to appreciate their moral dilemmas, to see why they thought and acted as they did, and why he, too, might have thought and acted likewise had he been in their situation. In a sense, the good historian "is always forgiving sins by the mere fact that he is finding out why they happened." [14]

Butterfield charged the Whig historians with trying to discover in previous ages the heroes and villains equivalent to modern day liberals and tories. Such efforts simplified both the uniqueness of every historical period and the complex causal movements whereby certain events and individuals in the past helped to shape the course of succeeding centuries. To claim that Luther was the forerunner of modern liberalism or Magna Carta the direct ancestor of the Glorious Revolution of 1688 was to ignore the subtlety of the historical process. For Butterfield, the ways of history were much more intricate than the moralistic, progress-oriented historians assumed. Whenever a sensitive historian undertook detailed research into a particular problem, he was likely to discover "the tricks that time plays with the purposes of men, as it turns those purposes to ends not realized." In setting out to build a uniform theocracy, for example, the seventeenth-century English Puritans unwittingly laid the ground for the spread of religious toleration and secularism; in their effort to build a fraternal, egalitarian utopia, Russian Bolsheviks wound up, to the horror of many of them, with a totalitarian regime ruled by a select few. The course of history was strewn with similar ironies, clues to the limits placed by reality upon the ideas and will of men, and to the unpredictability suffusing human action.[15]

The business of history was not to pinpoint the ideological forerunners of modern day movements and their respective heroes and villains but to study the subtle processes of historical change. "History is not the study of origins; rather it is the analysis of all the mediations by which the past was turned into our present."[16] As the historian began to study the devious ways whereby human purposes often brought about results vastly different from those intended, he would become aware of the dialectical texture of the historical process. This process was not a series of neat straight lines arranged in an orderly, logical fashion but a collage of conflicting patterns and colors which in their ceaseless clash produced unpredictable and ever new impressions. In such a collage, one observed "whig and tory combining in virtue of their very antagonism to produce those interactions which turn one age into another."[17] The course of historical change was not so much like a logical argument as a labyrinth. It was a process whose "mediations may be provided by anything in the world—by men's sins or misapprehensions or by . . . fortunate conjunctures. Very strange bridges are used to make the passage from one state of things to another. . . . their discovery is the glory of historical research."[18] In his efforts to see the past through the glasses of his moralistic categories, the Whig historian often would associate sixteenth-century Protestants with the advancement of progress and their Catholic adversaries with medievalism. According to Butterfield, however,

> instead of seeing the modern world emerge as the victory of the children of light over the children of darkness in any generation, it is at least better to see it emerge as the result of a clash of wills, a result which often neither party wanted or even dreamed of, a result which indeed in some cases both parties would equally have hated, but a result for the achievement of which the existence of both and the clash of both were necessary.[19]

In this passage one detects the idea of a balance of power, which played a major role in Butterfield's writings on international relations and which was an important aspect of his understanding of politics. If religious toleration and a degree of political pluralism became features of some European societies towards the end of the seventeenth century, it was not because one particular faction triumphed over another but precisely because none was able to impose its vision of order over the rest of society. In the ensuing tension and balance among competing forces and ideologies, institutions blending tradition with change and tolerance with religious faith began to flourish, bringing about something very different from what either Protestants or Catholics had fought each other to achieve.[20]

Rather than looking to the past to ascertain its similarity to the present, the historian must keep in mind the uniqueness of every historical moment and its attendant circumstances. In the study of history, "it is better to assume unlikeness at first and let any likenesses that subsequently appear take their proper proportions in their proper context." In order to understand the struggles between Protestants and Catholics in the sixteenth century, one had to consider the protagonists "as distant and strange people—as they really were—whose quarrels are as unrelated to ourselves as the factions of Blues and Greens in ancient Constantinople." If instead of appreciating the uniqueness of every historical moment we insisted on viewing the present as "an absolute to which all other generations are merely relative," we would lose "the true vision of ourselves which history is able to give." We would fail "to realize those things in which we too are merely relative, and . . . lose a chance of discovering where, in the stream of the centuries, we ourselves, and our ideas and prejudices," stood. It was important for the historian and the generation to which he belonged to realize that they were not the pinnacle towards which all previous history had moved. Those living in the present were "part of the historical process . . . not pioneers merely, but also passengers in the movement of things."[21]

Such humbling reflections were valuable in two respects. First, they could encourage a genuine interest in the past for its own sake and produce a historiography of integrity that refused to confirm current prejudices or look at past generations condescendingly. Second, they could remind us that the future, too, would be unique and somewhat unpredictable. No amount of careful tinkering on our part would imprison future generations in contemporary ideals, institutions, or historical patterns. While past circumstances and events conditioned the present to some degree, so that each generation was not as autonomous as it thought itself to be, every historical moment also had an element of unconditional freedom and the corresponding opportunity for those human beings participating in it to help shape their own destiny.[22] The course of history thus displayed a ceaseless tension between necessity and freedom, between familiar patterns of human action conditioned by previous historical currents and new historical developments that were the product of the human spirit and of that realm of human action which necessity and the past failed to determine.

The political implications of this way of thinking about history were important to Butterfield. Throughout the late 1940s and 1950s, while the

West was engaged in the dual struggles of decolonization and the cold war, he implored statesmen and citizens alike not to ascribe to the political clashes of the day transcendent significance. Important though they were, the challenges of the cold war should not be viewed with such intensity of feeling that one came to see the destinies of countless generations of mankind as dependent on their outcome. Indeed, one of the features of nuclear weapons that most disturbed Butterfield was the capability they gave to a generation or group of men for deciding the destinies of future human beings. The hitherto frustrated striving to shape the course of the political world long beyond one's life span, which Butterfield detected in the Egyptians and other ancient peoples, had a powerful instrument at its disposal in the late twentieth century. Faced with a Soviet ultimatum, a beleaguered United States president could say (and in this he would be reflecting the beliefs of millions of Americans), "rather than yield our descendants and ourselves to Soviet despotism, we will sacrifice their lives and ours in a nuclear holocaust." Similarly, a group of Soviet or American leaders, sensing that their side had achieved temporary strategic superiority, might decide on a risky, devastating first strike against the other power, so as to destroy forever the strongest obstacle to the achievement of world happiness. In either case, a small group of men would determine the future of successive generations with a frightening ironlike finality previously unknown in international politics.

In *The Whig Interpretation of History*, Butterfield warned against the dangers of drawing "lessons" from history. "The eliciting of general truths or of propositions claiming universal validity is the one kind of consummation which it is beyond the competence of history to achieve."[23] The historian's expertise and his tools were capable of deciphering only the particulars of history; as soon as he embarked on the task of searching for broad, universal generalizations or laws, his insights were no more valid than those of any intelligent layman involved in the same enterprise. This sharp distinction between technical history and philosophy of history may explain Butterfield's skepticism towards the grandiose theories of Arnold Toynbee, who resorted to his expertise as a technical historian to provide his philosophy of history with a corroboration that technical history was incapable of giving.

Butterfield's warning against deducing lessons from history, however, was more cautionary than peremptory. *The Whig Interpretation* was written to call into question the outlook and methods of a historiography where lessons abounded and where sweeping generalizations and supposed laws of progress smothered the particular and the unique in history. Later in his life, Butterfield obliquely admitted the value of looking to the past in search of wisdom. His extensive writings on diplomacy, the balance of power, raison d'etat, and international order attest his conviction that in the realm of practical politics one can profit from the experience of previous generations. As he wrote, somewhat complainingly, in a 1968 essay on morality and international politics, "because the problems and paradoxes of human relations show such constancies of fundamental pattern throughout the ages, it is the realm where man ought to learn most (though in reality he most refuses to learn) from the accumulated experience of the human race."[24] Indeed, Butterfield's emphasis in *The Whig Interpretation* on the role of necessity and conditioning circumstances suggested that it was possible to draw some lessons from history, even if such lessons were admittedly narrow in scope and subject to numerous qualifications and they had to be applied tentatively. A historical process whose contours were shaped by necessity and conditioning circumstances was bound to display continuities, recurrent patterns, and a degree of predictability throughout successive time periods.

If in later writings Butterfield modified his thesis about the difficulty of drawing lessons from history, he never wavered in his strong belief that it was improper for the historian to make moral judgments. *The Whig Interpretation*'s last chapter was an attack on the view of Lord Acton (1834–1902), one of England's foremost nineteenth-century historians and a predecessor of Butterfield at Cambridge, that "the office of historical sciences [is] to maintain morality as the sole impartial criterion of men and things."[25] Acton, the epitome of the Whig historian, was anxious to buttress contemporary morality and political ideas through the study of history; for him, the past was not an end in itself but a great lesson to the present generation on the crimes and evils of which man is capable and on the inherent wickedness of certain political principles. Moral judgments in history were an indispensable aid to man's political enlightenment and moral rectitude. "To develop and perfect and arm conscience is the great achievement of history," said the great historian.[26]

Acton's exalted view of the relationship of morality to history led him to an excessive rigorism in his moral judgments on historical figures. "Suffer no man and no cause to escape the undying penalty which history has the power to inflict on wrong," he once remarked. In contrast to Butterfield's suggestion that the historian learns to forgive sins as his understanding grows, Acton sternly warned, "Beware of too much explaining, lest we end by too much excusing." According to Acton, if the historian must err in his moral judgments he ought to err on the side of severity, not leniency. Throughout history, he argued, more evil had resulted from conscious sin and less from unconscious error than most people imagined.[27]

In stating his case against Acton, Butterfield did not question the validity of moral judgments but only the tendency of historians to use their technical expertise in history to give their moral opinions a sanctity this expertise could not provide. Before making moral judgments, the historian had to drop his mantle as historian and assume no greater authority for his conclusions than the rest of his fellow men. One of Butterfield's colleagues at Cambridge has captured for us some of the intensity and significance that the life-long dialogue with Acton had in Butterfield's life: "Although externally he conducted the argument as a public debate with Acton, it gave us all the sensation that we were privileged spectators of a private and engrossing debate within his soul—how historical understanding and moral conviction can be brought into harmony—when moral judgment corrupts the historians and yet moral judgment is of the essence of a man." [28]

Butterfield's main argument against Acton was that moral judgments were a barrier to historical understanding and therefore defeated the historian's foremost purpose. Whenever a historian made a definitive judgment on the wickedness or goodness of a particular person, he abandoned the pursuit of understanding; he brought to a halt what should be an unending task, the effort to delve deeper into the causes that prompted that person to think and act as he did. Moreover, the historian was incapable of entering into "the secret recesses of the personality where a man's final moral responsibility resides." [29] If this inability concerning the historian's own contemporaries were true, it was even truer of men and women centuries removed from him. Faced with this problem, the historian should not exonerate or condemn but only explain:

> Shall he condemn Mary Tudor as a persecutor and praise Catherine de' Medici for seeking toleration, or is it more true to say that Mary was fervent and consistent in her Catholicism, while Catherine was more worldly and indifferent? The historian's function is in the first place to describe the persecutions for which the English queen was responsible, and to narrate the attempts of the French queen to secure toleration; but because he has the art of sifting sources and weighing evidence, this does not mean that he has the subtlety to decide the incidence of moral blame or praise. He is the less a historian certainly if by any moral judgment he puts a stop to his imaginative endeavour, and if through moral indignation he cuts short the effort of historical understanding. Faced with the poisonings of which Alexander VI is accused, it is for the historian to be merely interested, merely curious to know how such things came to happen. [30]

As soon as the historian imagined himself capable of issuing authoritative moral judgments on the basis of the limited evidence available to him, he began to play God. Those who might accuse Butterfield of moral relativism should keep in mind that his injunctions against moral praise by historians were as strong as those against moral condemnation.

A serious problem confronting the historian bent on moral judgments was that of sifting necessity from freedom in human behavior, of ascertaining how much of a bad or good deed was due to the conditions facing the historical character and how much the result of goodness or evil within that person. In judging the character of Napoleon Bonaparte, for example, it was necessary to remember that as a rule he enjoyed almost boundless opportunities to exercise his willfulness and unlimited power to carry out his desires. In a similar situation, most of us might not have acted any more benignly or peacefully. To judge Napoleon as wicked by comparison with other statesmen was to overlook the important point that we never will know how a Castlereagh or a Pitt would have behaved if he had been in Napoleon's circumstances.

Butterfield's discussions of moral judgments in history, in *The Whig Interpretation* and later works, had important implications for his views on international politics. There was, for example, the emphasis on the pull of necessity and conditioning circumstances in the course of human affairs, a pull which became stronger and more difficult to transcend as one moved into the realm of politics and power. Acton himself recognized this pull when he wrote that "power tends to corrupt, and absolute power corrupts absolutely."

In his writings on international relations, Butterfield repeatedly contrasted the "scientific" with the "moralistic" approach to politics. By "scientific," however, he did not mean what many social scientists in Great Britain and the United States meant. Like Martin Wight, Adam Watson, and other members of the British Committee on the Theory of International Politics, Butterfield was highly skeptical of the various forms of behaviorism that have gained prominence in the social sciences over the last few decades. Behaviorism's impulse to reduce politics to quantifiable processes only could produce an incomplete picture of international affairs. Behaviorism left out the unique and the particular in history, those novel, unforeseeable developments that are the fruits of the human spirit. By downplaying those aspects of reality beyond the confines of its limited methodological tools, behaviorism failed to take into account the subtle "imponderables" of the political world which play such a crucial role in international politics. In reference to this problem, Butterfield kept warning the technical historian, as he had done in *The Historical Novel*, not to overlook the transempirical dimension of history and to pay some attention to "the poet, the prophet, the novelist and the playwright" who "reconstitute life in its wholeness."[31]

For Butterfield, the scientific approach to politics was simply a dispassionate examination of the workings of power and an imperfect environment upon a flawed human nature, one of its premises being Acton's wise recognition of the downward pull of power on even the best of men. The scientific approach was similar to technical history at its best, because it inquired into the processes of politics for the purpose of elucidating how war, peace, diplomacy, and an international order functioned instead of asking which wicked or saintly statesman or nation must be blamed or praised for this or that event. The moralistic approach, on the other hand, was similar to Whig historiography in its insistence on moral judgments, its eagerness to detect an upward, progressive march in international politics, and its tendency to cast nations and statesmen in the camp of the devil or in that of God's angels.

Butterfield thus gave a curious turn to his Augustinian view of human nature. No less than Acton, he was well aware of universal sinfulness. But, whereas this awareness led Acton to searing moral criticism of particular historical figures, for Butterfield it was an incentive to look underneath the vast catalog of human crimes and vices and discover the differences in human behavior as well as the circumstances responsible for such differences. The question was not whether Bismarck was more virtuous than Napoleon but whether, assuming both men to be sinful and prone to cupidity, a historian could go on to discover how and why one of them had embarked on a course of absolute mastery and the other on a course of political self-restraint. In other words, the idea of universal sinfulness was a foundation for a truly scientific approach to politics. It described accurately the most pervasive characteristic of human nature, constituting a safeguard against the kind of historiography and political analysis which judged some statesmen and nations as inherently more wicked than others, without searching for the mechanisms and conditions that propelled them to their deeds. Starting from the assumption of universal sinfulness, Butterfield was free to leave the moral issue behind and engage in such an inquiry.

Like the technical historian, the statesman must set the moral issue aside when he tries to understand the behavior of other states. His task is not to deplore or admire the moral level of other states and their leaders but to deal with them so as to further his country's interests; as Butterfield well knew, this task requires a dispassionate appraisal of political realities, a mind unclouded by the passion of moral judgments. The statesman can no more banish evil and evildoers from the world of international politics than the historian can banish them from the course of history. Both of them work with an asperous reality resistant to moral transformation and requiring understanding before moral evaluation.

In seeking to protect his country, the statesman must inquire into the causes of war without succumbing to the easy moralism that ascribes wars to the evil of a particular state or its leaders. An understanding of war must include a sensitivity to the correlation of forces and other conditions that give some states the opportunity, and others the obligation, to make war. In a fashion reminiscent of the technical historian, the statesman will ask himself how France, considered an enemy of the peace during the eighteenth and much of the nineteenth century, has come to be a guardian of international order in our times, while the Soviet Union, once our trusted ally, appears to have become an expansionist power in the aftermath of World War II. As the statesman poses these questions, he gains a more profound understanding of international politics. He begins to appreciate, for example, the importance of the balance of power and to perceive that in international politics the proper distribution of forces is a more reliable guarantee of peace than any amount of good intentions or moral rectitude.

The statesman's highest instrument is not moral rhetoric or prophetic righteousness, but diplomacy. Like technical history, diplomacy demands as its prerequisite the ability to put oneself in the other party's situation and perceive reality as the other party perceives it. This is one of the highest exercises in the scientific approach to politics. Unlike President Roosevelt in his dealings with Stalin, a skillful diplomat would not have relied on a leader's goodwill or his own charisma for the restraint of a state's ambitions. Instead, he would have worked towards circumstances, both political and military, in which the Soviet Union would have no temptations for expansion that would conflict with Western security. Our imaginary diplomat-statesman will not demand self-righteously that the Soviet Union give up the aspirations of a great power that his own country, be it Great Britain or the United States, enjoys. What he must do is provide room for those aspirations in a setting in which they do not threaten the West, while making it very risky for the Soviets to expand in areas vital to the West such as Europe or the Middle East.

In this extremely difficult endeavor, a diplomat will be most effective when, through the exercise of imagination and generous sympathy, he puts himself in the shoes of the Soviet leaders and sees the world as they do. Only then does the diplomat understand the genuine aspirations of the Soviet Union and, equally important, the right kinds of power and persuasion necessary to channel those aspirations along lines not inimical to Western interests. Our diplomat-statesman will avoid the self-righteousness of a John Foster Dulles, as well as the equally dangerous illusion of a Franklin D. Roosevelt. To this degree technical history and diplomacy are similar, in that they try to leave the moral issue behind and understand how a particular process, be it historical or political, takes place. The important difference, however, is that the historian only needs to understand, while the statesman must use the understanding gained through openness and a creative imagination to mold political reality on behalf of his state's interests. As will be discussed later with reference to Butterfield's study of the origins of World War I, he believed that in the field of foreign affairs the best statesmen are those who strive to maintain in their thinking and actions the difficult tension between the demands of detached understanding and those of protecting their people, using each set of demands in the service of the other.[32]

In his sensitivity to the interplay between universals and particularities in the study of history, his reluctance to pronounce moral judgments as a historian, and his awareness of the relationship between history and international politics, Butterfield was following in the footsteps of Leopold von Ranke (1795–1886), Germany's leading nineteenth-century historian. Ranke's influence on Butterfield's historical thinking was far-reaching. In 1955, a quarter of a century after *The Whig Interpretation of History* and in the train of numerous other historical, political, and religious writings, Butterfield published *Man on His Past*. A study of the development of historiography from the Göttingen School of the mid-eighteenth century down to the efforts of Ranke and Acton in the nineteenth, this work was also a running debate between the contending approaches of these two great historians to some of the profound philosophical issues and technical problems posed by their discipline. Besides serving as mediator between Acton and Ranke, emphasizing their common perspectives as well as their differences, Butterfield brought his own viewpoint into play. Here one appreciates again Acton's hold on Butterfield's imagination; if Butterfield repeatedly disagreed with Acton, it was because of the tremendous respect he had for him and because he knew there was much of value to be learned from his Cambridge predecessor. The extensive commentaries on Ranke contained in this work are doubly valuable to the readers. In the process of elucidating Ranke's views, Butterfield revealed the extent to which his own had been shaped by his unceasing dialogue with the German scholar one century removed from him.

In *Man on His Past* Butterfield softened his earlier thesis about the difficulty of drawing lessons from history and explained that the study of history required paying attention to details as well as to generalizations. While the historian constantly had to be on the lookout for the unique, he could not help but make generalizations and indicate broad trends. If "we push the doctrine of the unique individual and the unique episode too far, we only end by making it impossible to reflect on the past." In that case, "statesmen could never learn anything from history, for every political episode would be a law unto itself; and human beings could never learn anything from experience." He remarked that "the quality of the unique in every individual or event or moment is to be fully maintained; and yet the movements of masses and the processes of centuries can be the subject of generalization . . . history is a more difficult subject than some people realize because both these aspects of the matter have to be provided for."[33]

According to Butterfield, Ranke exhibited the same dual concern for the particular and the general in history. Ranke began his enterprise, however, as a revolt against the vast philosophical systems of the Enlightenment and Hegel which sought to imprint on history a shape dictated by abstract ideological principles rather than actual historical research. It was only natural that, in his revolt against the domination of history by ideology, Ranke, as Butterfield did in his attack on Whig historiography, would emphasize initially the importance of the unique in history. In Butterfield's words, Ranke felt "a joy in detail as such . . . a passion for human beings in themselves, in spite of their contradictions, and a love of events in their very uniqueness." [34]

Like Butterfield, Ranke pointed to the unique in history to cast doubt both on the effort to ascribe to the course of history a rationality it did not have and on the implication that the march of history was the march of progress, with all previous generations being but a stepping stone to a future culmination of humanity. Ranke stated the case against progress in history in the strongest possible manner: "nothing in the world . . . can ever be regarded as existing merely for the sake of something else." As he put it, somewhat poetically, all generations of humankind are equidistant from God. [35] Obviously agreeing, Butterfield wrote of Ranke that

> he is ready to admit that in the course of time an improved moral standard may gain wider currency amongst larger classes of society; but to him there is no progress in ethics beyond the morality of the New Testament. In our time more people may benefit from the stable conditions in which it is fairly easy to live a sober and respectable life. But the present day does not excel the world of over a thousand years ago in examples of spiritual depth or in the moral strength that grapples with great difficulties and temptations. [36]

At the same time, it was a misinterpretation of Ranke to charge him with loving merely isolated facts. According to Butterfield, Ranke also insisted on generalizations, demanding only that they issue out of the facts. History, said Ranke, "never has the unity of a philosophical system . . . but it is not at all . . . without interconnectedness." [37] Ranke's mind constantly strove to discover the links and continuities in history. His final objective was a universal history written by historians rather than by philosophers. He sensed that if the historians did not undertake this task of relating the particular to the general, in Butterfield's words, "some H. G. Wells will carry it out, and will acquire undue power over the minds of men" through philosophical presuppositions disguised as historical truth. [38] In displaying that tension between the unique and the general which should characterize all sound historiography, Ranke did "justice to free will and necessity, to what is unique and what can be generalized, to personality as something always valid in itself and to the kind of movements which are suprapersonal." [39]

Like Butterfield, Ranke perceived in history the tension between necessity and freedom, between conditioning circumstances and the spontaneity born out of the human spirit. Ranke could not accept liberalism's assertion of the inevitability of progress in history because, if such a predetermined end as progress was imposed on man from the outside, it meant that man had no free will; on the other hand, if progress came from something innate in man, then man was God, an equally false conclusion. According to Butterfield, Ranke believed that "the free choices of free men" have a real part in the making of history and that "God has left open to the future a multiplicity of alternative possible developments." In explaining Ranke's view of the relationship of freedom and necessity in the course of human affairs, Butterfield was describing his own view:

> What we ourselves do here and now will make a difference to the course which the future is to take; but involved in this is a process, the laws of which are not only unknown to us, but are more secret and profound than we can understand. In a sense, says Ranke, every individual must be regarded as free; and we must assume that at any moment something original may emerge—something which comes from the primary source of historical action, inside human beings. At the same time all the parts of history are interwoven—they condition one another and have their constant repercussions on one another. In this sense, freedom and necessity, he tells us, are rubbing shoulders at every moment.[40]

Ranke's historiography affected his view of international politics. His rejection of the progressive interpretation of history led him, as with Butterfield, to an interest in the traditional mechanisms of European power politics. For Ranke, limited war, the balance of power, diplomacy, and the Great Powers were not retrograde evils but instruments through which the European states preserved their independence and maintained a semblance of order in an imperfect world. He traced the development of the modern states-system and of the balance of power in his researches on European history from 1492 to 1789. In his famous essay "The Great Powers," he outlined the role played by a few leading European nations in keeping Europe free from the control of a single state. Like Butterfield, Ranke "adhered to the idea of a multiplicity of states which should stand approximately in equilibrium with one another. He did not want unity but gloried in the variety of nations," arguing that if there had been a single European state the cultural and spiritual heritage of Europe and the world would have been poorer.[41]

Ranke also elaborated the thesis of the primacy of foreign policy. In his study of history he detected the important role of international politics in marking the beginning and end of various historical periods, in determining the dominance of particular cultures and civilizations, and in shaping the internal political arrangements of states. Some of Ranke's successors, notably

Heinrich von Treitschke, transformed this insight into the rigid doctrine that the struggle for power and the victory of the strong over the weak are the quintessential themes of history.

As evidence for the primacy of foreign policy, Ranke pointed, for instance, to the rise and fall of the Roman Empire and the conquests of Alexander the Great as great landmarks in the history of antiquity. Butterfield agreed with Ranke that "these vast aggregations of power are momentous things in the history of civilization." Ranke also cited the golden age of Spanish art and literature in the sixteenth and early seventeenth centuries and the splendor of French culture during the reign of Louis XIV as evidence that political and military power are prerequisites for cultural dominance. Butterfield recalled his initial shock at Ranke's belief that, even when Goethe's contribution was taken into account, German culture gained its great momentum with the rise of German power and political confidence in the nineteenth century. Yet, with certain reluctance, he agreed with the German historian; reflecting on the cultural leadership which the United States and the Soviet Union had come to enjoy after World War II, Butterfield was "staggered to see how such matters are affected by a mere redistribution of power."[42]

Another of Ranke's arguments for the primacy of foreign policy was the close relationship he detected between a state's foreign policy and its internal constitution. An expansionist state with a successful foreign policy was more likely to develop absolutist institutions at home than one whose external failures weakened its domestic authority and legitimacy. France's foreign policy failures, according to Ranke, helped to precipitate the revolution of 1789. One of Ranke's successors, the twentieth-century German historian Ludwig Dehio, sharpened the focus of Ranke's thesis by contrasting insular and continental states and the effects of their different foreign policies on their domestic structures. Insular states, such as Venice, Great Britain, and the United States, were somewhat sheltered from the ruthless struggle of international politics and were able to develop free economic and political institutions. Continental states, on the other hand, were surrounded on all sides by competitive, hostile powers, their foreign policy had little margin for error, and, in these circumstances, internal cohesion and outer security became overriding values on behalf of which pluralism and liberty had to be sacrificed.[43]

To the extent that neither Ranke nor Dehio intended his observations to be rigid laws but only a demonstration of the indissoluble link between a state's internal development and the vast external realm of international politics in which that state must function, Butterfield agreed. He observed that, in English history, the great constitutional concessions were wrested from kings such as John, Charles I, or James II, all of whose foreign policy had been unusually unsuccessful. In our own century, two world wars with their massive displacements of power "were largely responsible for the success of communism over one great part of the globe, and the speeding up of egalitarianism over another great area." In justice to Butterfield and Ranke, it cannot be denied that the external Soviet threat has been a remarkable incentive to Western societies to reform their internal economic, social, and political institutions toward a greater degree of equality and participation.[44]

The observations of Ranke and Dehio are two aspects of the same thesis. Ranke suggested that, for constitutionalism to arise, a state's foreign policy must not be too successful, too expansive; only then are the rulers forced to look inwards and base their rule on the consent of the governed rather than their foreign exploits. While agreeing with Ranke, Dehio said that a state must have some security in order to develop any institutions of liberty at all; foreign policy catastrophes, if serious enough, do not bring about liberty but dictatorship, while a state sheltered from foreign dangers may look inwards, too, and develop free institutions. With reference to a contemporary state such as the Soviet Union, this could mean that the West's policy towards it would have to oscillate between, on the one hand, assuring the Soviet Union of its security and, on the other, thwarting Soviet expansionist efforts that might strengthen the regime's internal grip and render economic and political reforms in the direction of an open, pluralistic society unnecessary. Obviously, such calibration is highly difficult in practice.

Behind Ranke's ruminations on the primacy of foreign policy, Butterfield saw a realistic recognition of the workings of power in human affairs. Butterfield, however, thought that many subsequent historians had carried Ranke's point further than Ranke had intended, for Ranke also was aware of the intrinsic vitality of religion, morality, and culture. At the heart of Ranke's conception of history was an unceasing dialectical movement encompassing the opposite polarities of power and the free human spirit. Historical development involved not only "the rivalry of nations engaged in conflict with each other for the possession of the soil or for political supremacy," but also "those immortal works of genius in poetry and literature, in science and art, which . . . represent what is common to all mankind."[45] In his *History of the Popes*, Ranke stressed that brute force alone never could achieve anything positive in history. In all this, Butterfield agreed with Ranke and was even more emphatic. For Butterfield, the two most significant landmarks in the history of Western civilization were the victory of Christianity and the Scientific Revolution.[46] Both events suggested that, occasionally, mighty power structures are helpless in the face of the movements of the human spirit; after an unsuccessful struggle, power gives up its efforts to destroy such a movement, and instead tries to co-opt it into its designs.

Butterfield was quick to point out that the view "that moral agencies must be in co-operation with power before this latter can achieve anything of consequence in the world" had its pitfalls. Not all morality is good morality. "The case of Prussia in the nineteenth century and Russia in the twentieth may make us wonder . . . whether the so-called 'moral' factor is really the same thing as morality." Power may call to its assistance such cultural and moral values as the defense of civilization, patriotism, or courage in the pursuit of immoral or evil ends.[47]

Because Ranke conceived the possibility of power and the moral factor working together towards truly moral ends, he was tempted sometimes, as in his history of Prussia, to glorify the triumphs of power and assume a bit indiscriminately that power allied with "moral" forces would produce morally good results. Two other giants of nineteenth-century historiography, Lord Acton and Jacob Burckhardt, were deeply suspicious of the corrupting influence of power and of efforts to downplay the tension between the demands of political power and those of transcendent morality. Thus, they were safeguarded from Ranke's weakness in this respect. But all three historians, according to Butterfield, "agreed that, the world being constituted as it is, even power can perform a good function in society, when it imposes peace and establishes order over a wide region, thereby enabling the work of civilization to proceed and creating a field within which men may grow in reasonableness."[48] This was also Butterfield's view. His incisive understanding of the dark side of power never led him to lose sight of the beneficial role which power can play by bringing about a measure of organization and harmony indispensable to civilization and the growth of humane social and political institutions.

The tension that Butterfield perceived in the course of human events between conditioning circumstances and the force of human personality, and within human personality itself between man's lust for power and the beckoning of transcendence expressed in religion, morality, and art, underlay his analysis of Marxist historiography. Unlike numerous contemporaries who, during the twenties and thirties, eagerly embraced Marxism to discard it later amidst bitter disillusionment, Butterfield never felt any great temptation toward the Marxist alternative. It was not only that, in the words of a colleague, he considered Marxism "vaguely un-Yorkshire," alien to his most deeply held beliefs; to the young Butterfield of *The Historical Novel*, *The Peace Tactics of Napoleon*, and *The Whig Interpretation of History*, Marxism was also an impoverishing, if not outright unacceptable, form of reductionism which did violence to the dazzling richness of history. Perhaps because he never was a true believer in it, however, Butterfield displayed towards the Marxist interpretation of history a dispassionateness lacking in many of those whose fervent belief had turned into sour despair. In 1933 he expressed his views in an article, "History and the Marxian Method," published in *Scrutiny*. The analysis of Marxist historical thought presented here remained largely unchanged throughout the rest of his life.[49]

Butterfield began with the assumption that "men who work upon history are themselves partly moulded by it in the first place, conditioned by it even at the moment when they imagine themselves most free." There is "an historical process which, though not self-existing and self-acting, operates at any given moment, conditioning men and yet perpetually conditioned by them." In emphasizing the role played by economic conditions in shaping human behavior and institutions, Marxism offered historians a valuable insight which, however, was not as novel as many Marxists claimed; after all, in his masterful comparative study of regimes in the *Politics*, Aristotle had drawn attention to the major influence of economics, as had Thucydides in *The Peloponnesian War*. To those repulsed by the Marxist materialist framework, Butterfield explained that "a person can hold an economic interpretation of history without in any sense denying the existence of a spiritual element in life; for the interpretation is to be regarded rather as a thesis concerning the kind of universe in which the spirit has to work." In other words, an economic interpretation of history need not mean "that man can live by bread alone; on the contrary it carries rather the implication that . . . man, however spiritual he may be, cannot live without bread."[50]

Marxism also reminded historians of the role of conflict in history. As Butterfield himself had argued in *The Whig Interpretation* and elsewhere, history did not proceed by a logical development, along a straight line. Instead, movement occurred "because of the issues that perpetually arise within a given society . . . the issues lead to conflict . . . until the conflict itself brings men to the production of . . . a new world which may embrace or transcend" the struggling parties. Although there were important differences, there were also some points of similarity between Butterfield's view of historical evolution and the Marxist notion of dialectic.[51]

The Marxist emphasis on the social and economic roots of historical change was equally salutary:

> The Marxists . . . more than anybody else, have taught us to make our history a structural piece of analysis—something which is capable of becoming more profound than a piece of ordinary political narrative. Instead of stopping with a drama of personalities, Charles I fighting Cromwell for example, we move further to a kind of geological study, we try to see what was happening below the surface, we envisage the stresses and strains that take place in the structure of the whole country.[52]

Insofar as Marxism gave to the historian "the healthy reminder that his story ought to hug the soil and be near to earth," it was a valuable corrective to that historical idealism which divorced the course of politics, ideology, and religion from economic and material circumstances:

> When Napoleon said that the nature of the weapons decides every-thing else in the art and organisation of war; when Parry showed how the nature of instruments conditioned a development in music at an important point; when Holland Rose described how men opened their minds quickly enough for the great voyages of dis-covery once the requisite nautical apparatus was at their service; when Virginia Woolf gave £500 a year and a room of one's own as a necessary condition for the production of literature . . . they possessed what I mean by the right kind of feeling as historians. They realised that the grandest flights of the human mind are con-ditioned by the nature of the material universe in which the intel-lect has to work.[53]

For all its merits, however, the Marxist interpretation of history had serious defects of understanding "with which we must quarrel very radically indeed." The most fundamental of these was the materialist philosophy with which the Marxist interpretation of history unnecessarily had saddled itself. To pinpoint the importance of material conditions was one thing; to turn those into a complete, self-enclosed system of historical explanation was quite another. For most Marxists, "economic self-interest becomes not merely a bias inside human beings . . . not merely a fundamental feature of history . . . but the perpetual motor of men's activity and the standing subject of their mental calculations." Realist though he was, and deeply conscious of the pervasiveness of self-interest in human affairs, Butterfield nevertheless con-sidered the Marxist analysis a grand simplification. Marx's followers were "not sufficiently aware of the universe that lies inside a personality," not sen-sitive enough to man's quest for transcendence which could not be neatly ex-plained by the laws of economic necessity. Marxists and other historicists who dismissed a human being or an entire generation as simply the product of the age did violence to the uniqueness of human personality:

> All the influences and ingredients of a given age and environment are by no means sufficient in themselves to explain the next stage of the story, the next turn of events. These influences and ingre-dients are liable to be churned over afresh inside any human per-sonality, each man assimilating them, combining them and react-ing to them in his peculiar way. The result is that nobody is to be explained as the mere product of his age; but every personality is a separate fountain of action, unpredictable and for ever capable of producing new things. In a sense, each separate human being rep-

resents something that for the historian is irreducible—himself the possible source of a new stream in history. It is not a disembodied idea, as some men have thought, and not an economic factor, as Marxists assert, but the incalculability of a human personality that is "the starting-point of historical change." [54]

Marxist historiography rightly underlined the links between changes in the modes of production and the transformation of political and social institutions. But, whereas this analysis could be useful with reference to large-scale historical transitions that took place over "long stretches of time," it was inappropriate for explaining short-term historical developments with which historians were concerned most of the time. Marxist historiography could yield valuable insights in a comparative study of twelfth-century and nineteenth-century England, but its near obsession with economic causality made it an inadequate tool for studying the rise and fall of Napoleon Bonaparte, the diplomacy of the Concert of Europe, or the intricate complexities behind the seventeenth-century Puritan Revolution. As usual, Butterfield was deeply suspicious of any attempts, by Marxists or anybody else, to trace historical change to a single, unified cause. "In history," he wrote, "things become so entangled with one another, forces and factors so intricately interwoven, that it is difficult to take even the first steps in the delicate work of their unravelling." [55]

Some of the issues in Butterfield's critique of Marxist historiography figured prominently in another vigorous debate during the fifties. This time Butterfield's opponents were the eminent historian Sir Lewis Namier and his students, who sought to introduce into their studies of George III's reign many of the quantitative and behaviorist methods that were gaining prominence in the social sciences. The centerpiece of Namier's historiography was the concept of "the structure of politics." The play among vested economic interests of competing factions and the struggle for power as a means to financial reward were the scaffolding of politics, the unifying idea that provided coherence of interpretation in the historical study of late eighteenth-century British political life. Namier and his students buttressed their arguments with voluminous statistical studies purporting to measure and show a correlation between the exercise of corruption and patronage on one hand and the election patterns and voting behavior of members of Parliament on the other.

While praising the Namier school for "the massiveness of its detailed researches" and admitting that its members were "a formidable squadron for any critic to have to face," Butterfield did not hesitate to throw down the gauntlet. The effort to guide historical research along the narrow lines offered by Namier's disputable "structure of politics" was, typically, abhorrent to Butterfield. Furthermore, statistical techniques, while not undesirable in themselves, could only make matters worse in this case by leaving out unquantifiable but vital dimensions of political life. He complained:

> We hear too much about structure and vested interests, and too little about those higher political considerations which clearly enter the case at these important points in the story, and which help to turn the study of history into a political education. In fact, it is just here that, over and above the irrationalities of the world, the social pressures and the sheer play of forces, there moves something of rational purpose, something of the conscious calculations of reasoning and reasonable men. . . . over and above the structure of politics, we must have a political history that is set out in narrative form—an account of adult human beings, taking a hand in their fates and fortunes, pulling at the story in the direction they want to carry it, and making decisions of their own. We must have the kind of story in which (no matter how much we know about the structure of politics and the conditions of the time) we can never quite guess, at any given moment, what is going to happen next.[56]

Butterfield argued that it was precisely on the great constitutional issues of the day, on matters of the highest political import, that members of Parliament were most likely to vote according to their conscience and beliefs, disregarding the pull of factional loyalties and corruption. Hence, the Namier school's focus on party interests and patronage, while useful perhaps in revealing voting patterns on minor issues, was inadequate for providing an understanding of the momentous political and constitutional struggles of George III's reign. Historians needed to take seriously political philosophy as expressed by the leading ideas of the day. They could not simply dismiss the parliamentary speeches of Edmund Burke and Charles James Fox, or the declarations of the monarch himself, as mere rhetorical disguise for the naked clash of vested economic interests. The exercise of reason and the pursuit of normative imperatives played as important a role in politics as did cupidity, the lust for power, and the fragmentary chaos of competing interests. The Namier debate thus demonstrated the breadth and depth of Butterfield's understanding of man and his political life. In politics, as elsewhere, bad motives mixed with good ones; the pursuit of self-interest was accompanied by service to a higher good; and the unpredictability and fragmentariness suffusing all human existence did not prevent reasonable statesmen from occasionally altering the course of politics along a more creative and beneficial course.

4

The prophecies of the historian

Among twentieth-century historians, Butterfield stands out for that creative synthesis of political realism and traditional Christian theology on which he rooted his philosophy of history. Although he consistently warned historians not to confuse philosophy of history with technical historical research, he did not hesitate to put forward his own philosophical interpretations of the course of human events as he saw it. Writing as a political realist and a Christian, Butterfield argued that even though his philosophy of history lacked the scientific precision or corroboration generally available to the historian for the ascertainment of facts, it could nevertheless serve as a valuable paradigm for the study of political reality, a source of valuable insights for the historian, the political theorist, and the statesman. In other words, even someone unpersuaded of the validity of Butterfield's theological assumptions could find in his philosophy of history useful guideposts for a morally and politically sound statecraft. The core of this philosophy was presented in a series of lectures, which drew some of the largest audiences in the history of Cambridge University, in the Michaelmas term of 1948. They were subsequently published in 1949 as *Christianity and History*, one of Butterfield's most widely read books, which has been translated into eight languages. It was acclaimed by the *Times Literary Supplement* as "the most outstanding pronouncement of the meaning of history made by a professional historian in England since Acton's inaugural."

Since, to paraphrase Whitehead, the development of Christian philosophy of history in the West can be described as one long footnote to Augustine's *City of God*, the uniqueness of this aspect of Butterfield's work lies mainly in his treatment and application to twentieth-century political problems of two themes: Providence and judgment. With regard to the first, Butterfield helped to bring back into Protestant political discourse the notion of Providence, which had suffered heavy blows at the hands of Voltaire and other subsequent modern thinkers. He believed that God was sovereign over the course of history and that in the exercise of this sovereignty He made use of the whole range of human agencies. In His care of the world, God did not so much impose His will against the wills of man as He worked through man's actions to bring about His purposes. This divine reconciliation of the divine sovereign will with the free wills of man was Providence.

In his concept of Providence, Butterfield was partly indebted to Lord Acton, who also infused a strong notion of Providence into his historical interpretations. The main difference between the two seems to have been this: Acton saw Providence as insuring in history continuous progress, which he defined in terms of nineteenth-century classical liberalism; Butterfield, on the other hand, believed that Providence helped to remedy some of man's worst mistakes and to bring good out of evil but the fruits of Providence were not connected with any particular kind of political, economic, or social philosophy; insofar as human conventions evolved during the course of history, definitions of the political good and their concrete cultural manifestations also changed, so that the fruits of Providence could have different political, economic, social, and cultural forms.

Throughout the sad tale of human greed, lust for power, and conflict, Providence brought good out of evil, making, so to speak, the best out of the difficult circumstances within which it had to work. The source of this Providence was God's love for the world, hence the Christian could trust in it, although "we cannot make terms with it or demand that it give us either victory in war or exemption from cataclysm." While God's Providence did not insure the success of the righteous or an escape from nuclear holocaust, it did guarantee to the Christian "a mission in the world and the kind of triumph that may come out of apparent defeat—the kind of good that can be wrested out of evil." [1]

In these tentative wrestlings with the concept of Providence, Butterfield was trying to avoid the error of Marx, Hegel, and Christians such as Eusebius who claimed to have found an ultimate guarantee of the triumph in the realm of secular history of human aspirations for justice, peace, and happiness. For Butterfield the only guarantee, repeatedly vindicated throughout man's existence, was that "the light shineth in darkness, and the darkness comprehendeth it not." In the lowest depths of human suffering and destruction there was always a possibility of bringing forth some good; in the greatest of tragedies there remained opportunities for inner human regeneration and growth in wisdom. But there were no guarantees against sufferings and tragedy in history. This refusal to merge the whole of man's existence into history or to identify the meaning of man's life and the substance of his highest purposes exclusively with the course of social and political institutions seems alien to the prevailing secular ethos, which posits earthly success as the highest pinnacle of all human endeavors. But admiring readers of Fyodor Dostoevsky, Nikolai Berdyaev, and Alexander Solzhenitsyn cannot but respond favorably to Butterfield's treatment of the problem of suffering in history and the moral and intellectual courage required by his sober reading of the ways of Providence.[2]

An important dimension of divine Providence was what Butterfield called human providence. It was that whole realm of God's care for the world composed by the ideas, wills, and actions of man; it was the entire network of conscious and unconscious human interactions with, and responses to, God's purposes in history. He argued that "there is a Providence that we must regard as lying in the very constitution of things."[3] Every person who comes into the world finds himself in the midst of intricate patterns of political, moral, and social relationships which he did not create and cannot alter at will. In this fallen, chaotic world God allows patterns of order to evolve which throughout successive generations provide continuity and regularity in the course of human affairs. These numerous patterns of order have varied degrees of durability and usefulness, so that not all the components of the providential order are equally immune to change and eventual demise. The Roman Empire, or the feudal economic system, while serving in their time wide and useful purposes, were supplanted by other arrangements at the point when human cupidity, with all the resources of human creativity at its disposal, found a way to shatter the boundaries provided by the system. On the other hand, the ancient patterns of moral order embodied in the admonitions against the arbitrary taking of a person's life or goods, while often violated or hedged in with numerous exceptions, continue to play an authoritative role and to contribute to order in most contemporary societies.

As with divine Providence, the chief function of human providence is to create good out of the tragedy and evil of human existence:

> Whatever the ills of a generation—whether revolutions or wars or financial disasters—man's reconciling mind in the after-period will operate upon the ruins of the world that remain to it, making virtue of necessity, just as the great Fire of London or the destructive work of German bombers may lead to the creation of a finer city. . . . Let us praise, not revolution and war, but man's reconciling mind which acts the good fairy over the worst that human wilfulness may have decreed—which begins to play providence upon the past almost as soon as it has happened, redeeming the mistakes, changing evil into good and turning necessity into opportunity.[4]

Human providence is part of man's response to the beckoning of transcendence. Even in the darkest moments, man moves to affirm the presence of the divine image within him. Such an affirmation or response, as part of the network of relationships forming Providence, usually expresses itself in the imaginative fashioning of new patterns of order at different levels of human existence whereby we bring a measure of order, coherence, and purposiveness to our lives and institutions.

The dynamics of human providence are difficult to understand because they encompass the acts of human beings freely and consciously pursuing their goals, as well as the manifestations of God's will in history which can take multitudinous forms. While God is sovereign over history, He allows and takes into account in His designs as numerous a range of considerations as the exercise by man for good and evil of his creative moral, intellectual, and physical faculties; the entire spectrum of irrationality and disorder coloring human existence; and the whole set of conditioning circumstances shaping and limiting man's life in both time and space. If, as Butterfield said in his commentary on Ranke, freedom and necessity "are rubbing shoulders at every moment" in history, it is equally true that the divine and human dimensions of Providence are continuously interacting with one another producing a historical process "the laws of which are not only unknown to us, but are more secret and profound than we can understand."[5]

Butterfield claimed that even someone unable to accept the theological underpinnings of his understanding of Providence could profit from its political and historical implications. One need not be a Christian to acknowledge that the texture of history, past and present, is interlaced with a myriad of unpredictable enigmatic forces or that the course of human events often has its own direction and momentum which become obvious only in retrospect and which no single individual could have altered at will. Even secular-minded historians spend considerable time studying and trying to understand "that kind of history-making which goes on so to speak over our heads, now deflecting the results of our actions, now taking our purposes out of our hands, and now turning our endeavors to ends not realised."[6]

Three major implications of Butterfield's understanding of Providence, acceptable to believers and nonbelievers, are as follows. Man is not sovereign over the direction of history; the forces of historical change are far too numerous and insusceptible to rational control and their inner relationships too complex for man to assume that he can consistently steer such forces along a predetermined course. Second, no generation is ever able to achieve a total transformation of the patterns of order and limiting circumstances with which it finds itself surrounded. Third, man lacks complete control over the consequences of his own actions; hence, political leaders must appreciate the wide gap between the intentions and rational designs motivating their policies on the one hand and the surprising, often unrecognizable, results of those policies on the other, once they have been carried out. This was the kind of secular interpretation of Providence out of which, according to Butterfield, the eighteenth century derived its diplomatic theory and practice. As he explained:

> Though the minds of the eighteenth century were losing the religious idea of Providence, they clung very tightly to that purely secular conception of a providential order which I have already mentioned. They told themselves that they ought to be on guard against presumption when it was a question of a radical break with that providential order. Precisely because no human mind can compass all the factors or command the complexities, precisely because no man can predict the forces that may be let loose when the fundamentals of an existing system are uprooted, precisely because the slightest miscalculation might release the world upon a current of unforeseeable, uncontrollable change, the eighteenth century kept that conception of a providential order . . . which it was thought necessary in general to maintain—a conception which like a number of other things seemed to survive as a kind of shell after the religion, which had given it some reality, had evaporated out of it.[7]

During the course of the eighteenth and nineteenth centuries, theorists and practitioners of diplomacy such as Callières, Heeren, Burke, Gentz, Metternich, and Bismarck elaborated a series of maxims—not laws, but tentative counsels of practical morality to the statesman—which in their totality defined a form of diplomacy and statecraft designed to "co-operate with Providence," to work with existing patterns of order rather than against them:

> If there was a risk of producing a situation that would run out of control, it would be better even to keep an ancient frontier, though it was not perfect; for if a frontier has lasted hundreds of years, then it has at least got over one of the hurdles, has at least the virtue of custom on its side, whereas to have new men discontented and unsettled under the conditions of new frontiers—or at least to have too many of them in the world—might produce a danger more incalculable, as well as deranging the balance of forces over the whole continent. And the principles of the eighteenth-century science of diplomacy, which I am describing, would have regarded as an illegitimate interference with the providential order any deliberate attempt to go further than mere defeat and actually to destroy a great state—to wipe your enemy off the map; for the new disposition of forces which comes about when you destroy the enemy power altogether is bound to be still less calculable, still

less amenable to control. They took the line, therefore, that we ought never to forget that the enemy of to-day may be needed as an ally against some other power to-morrow; in other words, that wars should be regarded as quarrels between allies who happen to have fallen out.[8]

This was a statecraft of conservatism, in the finest sense of the word, in the tradition of Edmund Burke rather than of those late twentieth-century American conservatives eager to transform the world in the likeness of their great country. It was also a statecraft sharply cognizant of the limits of power. A stark existential humility colored its maxims, and perhaps no more apt examples of this humility could be found than in these words of Bismarck deeply treasured by both Butterfield and Henry Kissinger: "The statesman cannot create the stream of time, he can only navigate upon it . . . he must try and reach for the hem when he hears the garment of God rustling through events." Bismarck also had said, in response to the impatient prompting of many to hasten Germany's unification, "We can advance the clock but time itself does not move any more quickly for that. . . . An arbitrary and merely willful interference with the course of history has always resulted only in beating off fruits that were not ripe."[9]

Both Bismarck and Metternich realized that underneath the sophisticated edifice of the European society of states lay powerful, unpredictable forces of disorder, irrationality, and destruction, including ancient ethnic and political rivalries and the passionate lust for power and glory, which could be controlled only with great effort. The maxim of classical eighteenth- and nineteenth-centuy diplomacy outlined ways for statesmen to build on the existing international order, on the political arrangements and patterns developed over time that in their sum resembled a providential order inherited from previous generations. A diplomacy which ignored this order, or tried to alter it radically, launched the state and the international society within which it functioned on an unforeseeable course, risking the release of those primeval forces of chaos formerly kept within bounds. In particular, it risked destroying the consciousness of common interests, that elusive *reason of system*, which kept the European states from plunging into a fratricidal war of all against all in pursuit of an unrealistically narrow, short-term national interest. While the statesmanship sketched by the maxims of classical statecraft recognized the presence of unpredictability, irrationality, and self-interest in international relations, it tried to restrict their scope by introducing a measure of regularity and a sense of common interests in the conduct of foreign policy.

At the core of these maxims were the conduct of limited war for limited objectives; the exercise of political forgiveness and magnanimity toward defeated adversaries; the realization that the quest for absolute security, even by one's own state, was impermissible, as it was likely to create insecurity for everyone else; the avoidance of ideological crusades or "wars for righteousness"; the recognition that all members of the states-system had a right to belong to it regardless of whatever temporary quarrels might arise among them and regardless of religious, ideological, or other differences; the ability to place oneself in the position of other states and acknowledge the grievances, anxieties, and fears they might have concerning one's power; the avoidance of drastic territorial settlements or radical redistributions in the balance of power; the distinction between vital and nonvital interests and the ensuing willingness to pursue a flexible diplomacy that left one's state a line of retreat and avoided placing the adversary in a position from which it could not retreat without suffering humiliation; the conduct of policy with unflagging attention to its impact on the overall balance of power; and the subordination of military to political objectives. In disregarding some of these maxims, the peacemakers at Versailles in 1919, and perhaps even Great Britain and the United States during World War II, "played too high a game with Providence," according to Butterfield. The efforts to redraw Europe's boundaries or to humiliate and even annihilate a major power such as Germany, which traditionally had served as a buffer between Western Europe and Russia, were likely to create new political conditions and a distribution of forces less amenable to calculation and control than the older patterns of order.[10]

Butterfield drew a sharp contrast between the willingness supposedly displayed by many of the practitioners of classical diplomacy "to work with history," to "cooperate with Providence," and the arrogant "presumptuousness" of Napoleon, Hitler, Mussolini, and all those statesmen who have imagined that "they can control things in a sovereign manner, as though they were kings of the earth, playing Providence not only for themselves but for the far future . . . gambling on a lot of risky calculations in which there must never be a single mistake." He also was fond of comparing traditional British diplomacy with the foreign policy of post-Bismarckian Germany. Despite its blunders and occasional rigidity, British diplomacy had displayed sufficient flexibility, pragmatism, and preference for a step-by-step approach rather than the grand strategy, to avert total ruin, profiting "from the unexpected ways in which time and chance itself will occasionally throw in a helping hand."[11]

Post-Bismarckian Germany, on the other hand, had relied more often than it should have on bold and even reckless military and political designs whose success depended on "the ability to calculate all possible contingencies and absolutely hit the bull's eye," in flagrant disregard of the unpredictability

built into the fabric of human events. The famous Schlieffen Plan; the almost cavalier attitude of the High Command toward the danger of America's
entry into World War I; the subsequent race against time in which Germany
hoped to strangle Britain's supply lines, defeat Russia, and bring all the pressure of the German war machine on the Western front to achieve a smashing
victory before the American armies arrived in mass; and, in World War II,
Hitler's titanic two-front struggle—all were instances in which the Germans
"gambled everything on a colossal system of policy which, if it had been a
hundred per cent successful would have been brilliant in its results, but
which challenged time and circumstance too boldly in that if it succeeded
only ninety per cent . . . it utterly failed." [12] The proverbial British "mud-
dling through" was preferable to Butterfield as "a system which, if it was
sixty per cent successful, at least gave a sixty per cent return"; it was also a
way of conducting policy more in keeping with a world in which the course
of events is beyond the absolute control of a few human beings and where
flexibility, openness, and an awareness of one's limits are, therefore, prerequisites to good statesmanship. [13]

Implicit in Butterfield's understanding of Providence was an aversion to
all grandiose designs, in either domestic or foreign policy, which promised a
future Arcadian bliss in exchange for further blood and toil from those human beings living here and now:

> There is danger nowadays that one generation after another will be
> asked to lay itself on the altar for sacrifice, taught by the successive
> prophets of one utopia after another that this self-immolation will
> lead to a new heaven and new earth in the time, shall we say, of
> their great-grandchildren. And in such circumstances the sacrifice
> of the present generation of real live men is definitive and irre-
> trievable, while the utopia which is supposed to serve as the com-
> pensation for it is hypothetical at best, since it is remote and de-
> pends on the concurrence of other favourable factors, too. [14]

It was important "to leave the future flexible," to refuse the ancient and
ever-recurring temptation to lock the generations ahead into our relative
ideals. If "every generation of humankind was equidistant from God," their
dignity and integrity required that each of them be allowed to play their part
in deciding the great issues of human existence. Similarly, every generation
should be allowed to seek beauty, truth, and love in the world as it is and not
be made to wait for a supposed transformation of the human condition which,
given man's sinful nature, the vagaries of the historical process, and the sovereignty of God, it is impossible for man to bring about at will. From time
immemorial life

has been a case of plucking beauty out of dangerous crags and cre-
vices, and making sure that there should be music somewhere
though apparently the world was generally near the edge of the
abyss. And we must have our Elizabethan literature even though
the Spanish Armada may be coming, because it is always part of
the game that the good life must be attained now, no matter at what
date in history you place the "now".[15]

This was a subtle, yet bitter draught for any serious utopian. It was proffered
to those Marxists and fervent anti-Communists who insist that life should
not begin until the adversary is crushed, as well as to the pious Evangelicals
and social reformers for whom no Chartres should have been built, no Jo-
hann Sebastian Bach hired, until the last remnants of poverty are banished
from the world.

While elements of traditional Christian thought and the teachings of
eighteenth-century diplomacy played a major role in Butterfield's concept of
Providence, another significant contribution came from the essential traditions of English history as he understood them. Among all peoples in modern history, the English had been the most successful in embodying historical, political, and moral wisdom in their institutions and statecraft. They
had achieved this slowly over the course of the centuries in a process which
culminated in the flowering and eventual ascendancy in English life of the
Whig tradition in the late seventeenth and eighteenth centuries. For Butterfield, the Whig heritage, though loaded with its share of aberrations as he
had shown earlier in *The Whig Interpretation of History*, nevertheless had the
salutary effect of inculcating in the English a love for ordered liberty, political compromise, moderation, and gradualism well suited to the ways of Providence and the cragginess of the historical process.

Butterfield presented these ideas in *The Englishman and His History*
(1944), the first half of which, dealing with the development of the Whig
interpretation of history during the seventeenth century, had its origins in a
series of lectures he gave at the universities of Cologne, Bonn, Münster, and
Berlin in 1938. The second and more explosive half, tracing the influences
of Christianity and the Whig view of history on the Whig political tradition,
was written at the height of the war years. In Butterfield's unabashed praise
of the English political heritage, one hears the voice of a man who, for all his
injunctions to detachment, was aware of the profound moral issues at stake in
his country's struggle for survival; when the great crisis burst upon him in
the peaceable solitude of his academic refuge, he did not hesitate to remind
himself and his countrymen of the essence of England's finest contributions
to Western civilization.

Towards the last few decades of the seventeenth century, a small group of Whig politicians and pamphleteers had worked out a set of political practices which eventually spread throughout both the Whig and Tory parties, becoming the dominant tradition in English politics. Butterfield considered these practices the source of "the Englishman's genius for political adjustment, his aptitude for give-and-take, his inclination to compromise, his disposition to co-operate with the trend of events themselves, without too great fretfulness when these are not quite to his liking." He wrote:

> The tradition of the English whigs stood for a gradual, ordered progress, the kind that is conducted somewhat as opportunity allows or as necessity dictates. These men knew when it would be best to give way to the pressure of events. They seemed to understand—by tradition and instinct—how to co-operate with history. They did not attempt to force the pace unduly, for they held it as important, among other political objects, to prevent conflict from becoming too bitter or the situation from becoming desperate or events from running out of control. They knew that if they waited awhile, time and a growing reasonableness in men, or perhaps a change of circumstances, would enable them to carry their aim by means less sensational, less heavily charged with danger, less vulnerable to time's revenges. And they knew that there are some evils which . . . must be "stroked away rather than kicked away"; that, as we can only master nature by becoming somewhat its servant and its ally, so we can achieve things with our history, and our fate, only by a similar humility. The whig . . . leans upon events somewhat, and seeks to ally himself with the underlying trend of things.[16]

This was the Whig form of "co-operation with Providence." It was a variant of that kind of political thinking and practice counseled in foreign affairs by the maxims of eighteenth-century diplomacy. At the heart of the Whig's respect for Providence were an awareness of limits, an appreciation for the wisdom of the past and the continuities tying the past to the present, recognition of the adversary's humanity, a distrust of ideological extremes, and an acceptance of the wide gulf between moral and political abstractions on the one hand and practical moral and political wisdom on the other. This framework for the conduct of politics became a national patrimony, as much a part of the Tories' philosophy as of that of the Whigs, Edmund Burke being but one of its most gifted and articulate exponents. According to Butterfield, the English political tradition that evolved from the Whigs rested on a mildly optimistic view of history, a Christian view of human personality, and a conception of politics and ethics in which the limits to human action were well recognized:

Implicit in the system is what we might call a tempered faith in the course of history, provided men do the best they can with due regard to their limitations. Implicit also is the awareness of a ceiling that is not sky-high, a sense of the limited degree to which the ills of the world can be quickly remedied by politics. There is a feeling also for certain imponderable things, certain values difficult to define or locate perhaps, which are ours by the mere fact that we preserve so much of the continuity of our history. . . . This whole political outlook further implies a respect for the other man's personality, a recognition of what is due to political opponents, a certain homage to what the other man may think to be a political good. . . . The system that we have inherited from the whigs replaces the doctrinaire quest for the highest good by the more difficult search—the enquiry that demands so much more austere self-discipline—the pursuit of the highest practicable good. It implies even a reluctance to force an issue on the mere strength of a momentary acquisition of power. . . . All these things . . . mere feathers to the impatient armchair politician . . . are aspects of that self-limitation which is necessary for those who seek to co-operate with history.[17]

Butterfield's concept of Providence, derived from his interpretation of Christian theology, classical realist statecraft, and the Whig political tradition in English history, raises the important question of its usefulness to the statesman. True, the idea of Providence and its political implications will not always determine in advance which policies the statesman will choose and which ones he will refuse; the line between presumptuousness and that healthy boldness which can be a prerequisite for success is often a fine one. Yet, as Sir Winston Churchill has reminded us in his memoirs and history of World War II, on this distinction and its accurate perception lies one of the differences between foolishness and wisdom in statecraft. Butterfield's understanding of Providence, when assimilated by the statesman and used not as an infallible source of revelation but as a background for his political decisions, contributes to wisdom in statecraft by reminding the statesman of his limits, of the almost indomitable character of the historical forces with which he must work, and of the usefulness of biding his time, without excessive anxiety, until circumstances are favorable to his purposes.

Respect for Providence, for the sovereign work of God in history, implied what Butterfield called, with regard to the Whigs, a "tempered faith in the course of history." One of Butterfield's favorite maxims, taken from the Old Testament, was "fret not thyself because of evildoers." Much presumptuousness and many disasters in foreign policy could be traced to excessive fear and anxiety on the part of statesmen towards future possible or imagined contingencies. The existential serenity implied in an acknowledgement of Providence was not, of course, as some critics might charge, a passive fatalism or a propensity to drift wherever the tide of events went. It was rather a kind of quiet confidence, a reluctance to overplay one's hand, necessary to maintain the national will and purposes under the control of reasonable policies as opposed to the dominion of fear.

As the leader of the Western world and the possessor of both weapons of global destruction and the means for helping to build a better international order, the United States can profit from exercising the kind of statecraft suggested by Butterfield's understanding of Providence. The sad irony is that those who might be expected to be the staunchest advocates of such a statecraft, America's conservatives, are not such advocates today. For all their professed admiration towards Edmund Burke, Alexander Hamilton, John Adams, George Washington, and John Quincy Adams, American conservatives in the late twentieth century are too attached to the Messianic strand in their nation's heritage, too devoted to the Wilsonian dream of transforming the world in America's image, to accept the foreign policy of sober judgment, confident patience, and a discriminating exercise of power counselled by Butterfield and those great conservatives just mentioned.[18]

The usual reply to this charge is that today we live in a convulsed, revolutionary world in which Butterfield's concept of Providence and its concomitant high regard for the maxims of classical diplomacy are a recipe for disaster, an invitation to national suicide. What America needs, so the argument goes, is a vigorous assertion of its will with all the resources at its disposal, a foreign policy universalist and relentless in its objectives, daring in its methods, and swift in its execution, that will destroy Soviet power just in time to save our ever feebler Western civilization. In today's world there is no basis for any faith in the West's ultimate success, no reason for not fretting over all the evildoers, in the Soviet camp and the Third World, that seem to be multiplying with the passing of each decade. A bold, maximalist foreign policy is our best hope. This seems to be the underlying rationale, the unspoken assumption, behind much of the conservative thinking on American foreign policy, even when such thinking is not articulated as radically as it has been here.

Advocates of this line of argument, however, would do well to recall— as Butterfield indeed reminded them—that the foreign policy successes of America's greatest adversary, the Soviet Union, have been largely the result of precisely that confidence in the future and that cool, calculated restraint advised by Butterfield. Although officially disdainful of a religious concept of Providence, the Soviet Union has seized upon an equally effective secular parallel notion—the Marxist view of history—to give to its foreign policy a high degree of soberness and flexibility which Butterfield ascribed to the Soviets' belief that the future is on their side. As Butterfield explained in a 1949 letter to his close friend Adam Watson, the British career diplomat and Foreign Office expert on Russian affairs who edited Butterfield's *Origins of History* after his death,

> On purely diplomatic considerations the danger is greater than if the government of Russia had been as efficient as at present but still under the Tsars. I think this precisely because the Soviets may be less wilfully, childishly and capriciously aggressive than the Tsars. In other words they seem to share with the Vatican at its best periods in a policy which (leaving aside all question of dishonesties) is more long-term than anybody else's, and therefore, e.g., more elastic—the kind of policy which rests on the faith that the long future is with them. This means that not only now but over the last 30 years I have still to be convinced that Soviet diplomacy has not been far superior to ours—still to be convinced that they have been foolish when we have thought them foolish. I believe I am still to be convinced that they have made a large-scale mistake of the kind we have made so often—though they may have been too clever in the summer of 1939—but I am not even sure of that.[19]

As early as 1949 Butterfield discerned that, while Marxism has given to Soviet pronouncements and avowed purposes a revolutionary, reckless tone, it also has been the source in Soviet foreign policy of great prudence and political patience. When it comes to deeds, rather then rhetoric, it is difficult to match the Soviets in their caution, perseverance, and unwillingness to gamble away advantages already won in exchange for the pursuit of grandiose ideological crusades.

Another dimension of Butterfield's understanding of Providence that can be politically useful to American conservatives was his recognition of the destructive consequences of total war upon the mechanisms of international order and the social and political traditions and institutions of particular societies. Drawing upon his intimate knowledge of the Napoleonic wars in the nineteenth century and both world wars in the twentieth, Butterfield pointed to the breakdown of the providential order at the twin levels of international relations and the nation-state, to the disintegration of tradition, civilization, and reasonableness, and to the mushrooming of radical politics and policies, all of them set in motion by the pressures, demands, and frustrations of total war. Too often, statesmen erroneously had seen total war as a means of strengthening the existing institutions and patterns of order, rather than as the uncontrollable catalyst for upheaval that it is.

For all its defects, the contemporary international system is one in which the United States maintains its ability to protect its interests and way of life. At home American society continues to display that creative tension between order and liberty, between tradition and change, that has characterized it for the past two centuries. Any total war against the Soviet Union, any attempt to destroy our chief adversary once and for all so as to clear the way for a supposed new golden era of humankind, is likely to destroy those very values cherished by conservatives. A major war between the United States and the Soviet Union, such as is readily contemplated by high military circles in both superpowers, even if it were fought mostly with conventional weapons and did not lead to a nuclear Armageddon and even if it were won by the United States, would not necessarily lead to an Americanized world. The resulting expansion of Chinese power and the continuing development of regional centers of powers in the Third World, whose influence would only grow during a major superpower conflict, would be sufficient to make the postwar world as dangerous and unmanageable as it presently is, if not more so. Meanwhile, the values of limited government, a free economy, individualism, and moral order which conservatives treasure in our society would suffer also under the great pressures generated by the titanic struggle.[20]

Butterfield's warnings against excessive anxiety, daring gambles of presumptuousness in foreign policy, geo-political hubris, and ideological self-righteousness belong to an honorable tradition of conservative thought stretching from Edmund Burke, through Alexander Hamilton, George Washington, and John Quincy Adams, down to Winston Churchill. It is time that American conservatives adopted the way of thinking embodied in this tradition and incorporated it into their vision of America's foreign policy. As a great power with vast natural resources, encompassing a free society ruled through law and possessed of a heritage marked by great achievements in all fields of human endeavor, the United States can look to the future not with excessive anxiety or desperation but with quiet confidence. And this confidence, in turn, can lead to the kind of foreign policy, flexible, prudent, and sober, through which our adversaries have achieved some of their most striking successes in the past four decades.

Even for those unwilling to believe that the future is with the West, the observations of the Cambridge historian retain much meaning. As comes across very clearly in *The Peace Tactics of Napoleon* and other works, Butterfield suspected what many great historians from Thucydides onwards also have suspected: that in international politics survival and the preservation of one's way of life come in the long run to those who make the fewest, least damaging mistakes. In a turbulent, revolutionary era of world politics such as the United States will face for the foreseeable future, ultimate success will be the reward of those who, through their sense of limits, weather the storm with a combination of prudence and patience rather than any brilliant and aggressive gambles risking the loss of everything. One hopes that American conservatives will discover in these Butterfieldian insights the basis for a new foreign policy suited for the perilous decades ahead. The future of the United States and of Western civilization could well depend on such discovery.

All this, of course, should not obscure two important points. First, if Butterfield's work can serve as a corrective to some of the tendencies of contemporary American conservative thought, it is also a massive critique of the political sentimentalities of much of modern liberalism in the United States and elsewhere. Second, Butterfield did not claim to provide—nor has anyone else succeeded in providing—an answer to what is perhaps the most vexing question in international affairs, the problem of deciding when it is best to act forcefully and boldly in the protection of national interests and when it is preferable to opt for a patient strategy of conciliatory and sympathetic diplomacy. He thought that in most circumstances a blend of these two approaches was likely to yield the best results. Military strength and political resoluteness could provide one's diplomacy with a credible foundation, while the pursuit of negotiations and a long-term strategy of accommodation could prevent the unwise or wasteful use of one's military and political resources. As to the exact proportions in each unique situation, no specific or detailed answers were possible, and only prudence could dictate one's course of action. Perhaps no one has understood this dilemma better than Churchill. In his history of World War II, after he bitterly criticized Neville Chamberlain for the disastrous consequences of his Munich agreement with Hitler in 1938, Churchill reflected:

> Those who are prone by temperament and character to seek sharp and clear-cut solutions of difficult and obscure problems, who are ready to fight whenever some challenge comes from a foreign Power, have not always been right. On the other hand, those whose inclination is to bow their heads, to seek patiently and faithfully for peaceful compromise, are not always wrong. On the contrary, in the majority of instances they may be right, not only morally but from a practical standpoint. How many wars have been averted by patience and persisting good will! . . . How many wars have been precipitated by firebrands! How many misunderstandings which led to wars could have been removed by temporising! . . .

> . . . [The duty of ministers] is first so to deal with other nations as to avoid strife and war and to eschew aggression in all its forms, whether for nationalistic or ideological objects. But the safety of the State, the lives and freedom of their own fellow countrymen, to whom they owe their position, make it right and im-

perative in the last resort, or when a final and definite conviction
has been reached, that the use of force should not be excluded. If
the circumstances are such as to warrant it, force may be used.
And if this be so, it should be used under the conditions which are
most favourable. There is no merit in putting off a war for a year
if, when it comes, it is a far worse war or one much harder to win.
These are the tormenting dilemmas upon which mankind has
throughout its history been so frequently impaled.[21]

Clearly, the confidence in the future counselled by Butterfield was intended to be a source of restraint for the statesman, not one of
arrogance or foolish pride. Butterfield's belief that "there is a judgment of
God involved in the very processes of history" was bound to have equally
salutary effects: the instillation of a deep existential humility and moral sensitivity in the hearts and minds of political decision makers.[22]

The affirmation of the old biblical notion of judgment in the context of
the problems of twentieth-century international politics was, of course, not
uniquely Butterfieldian. Several of Butterfield's contemporaries, including
Christopher Dawson, Nikolai Berdyaev, Karl Barth, Martin Wight, and
Reinhold Niebuhr, reiterated this theme throughout their writings. Together with Butterfield, they belonged to a generation of Christian thinkers
who were highly skeptical of liberal Christianity and of that political liberalism which had held sway in the West during much of the nineteenth century and the early part of the twentieth. In its negation of sin and tragedy, its
attachment to the idea of progress, and its promise of the perfectibility of
human nature, liberal Christianity and its secular counterpart failed to do
justice to the catastrophic and terrible realities of the human condition as experienced by twentieth-century man. The debacle of World War I, the Bol-
shevik Revolution, the embodiment of irrationality in Fascist Italy and Nazi
Germany, the destruction of tens of millions of human beings at the hands of
Stalin and Hitler, the conflagration of World War II, and the development
and use of terrifying means of war, including nuclear weapons capable of
destroying human life forever, were all dark shadows that liberalism could
not explain and that compelled these thinkers to seek new answers in the old
tradition of biblical and Christian orthodoxy. As the Oxford historian Michael Howard writes:

> Christianity, unlike Liberalism or Marxism, did provide an
> explanation; not the cheerful liberal humanitarian Christian teach-
> ing which read little into the Bible except the Nativity and the Ser-
> mon on the Mount, but the teaching which digested all the im-
> plications of the Old Testament, including the prophetic books,

before turning to the New, which emphasised that the Gospels themselves were full of uncompromisingly dark passages, and which faced the fact that at the centre of the Christian religion, as of no other great world religion, was a symbol of prolonged and unavoidable suffering. The Christian eschatology, long disdained by liberal humanists even within the Church itself, once again became terrifyingly relevant to human affairs. The works of Charles Williams, of C. S. Lewis, and—drawing on yet wider sources of Manichean myth—of J. R. R. Tolkien were deservedly popular as allegorical commentaries on the events of the time. And the teachers who best provided an adequate framework for understanding were the philosophers and the theologians—Niebuhr, Bonhoeffer, Karl Barth, Tillich—who accepted uncomplainingly the remoteness, the inscrutability of God, who saw the focus of Christianity as the Passion rather than the Sermon on the Mount; men for whom the march of humanitarian, utilitarian liberalism, including its change of gear into Marxian socialism, had simply been a long excursion into the desert in pursuit of a mirage.[23]

Butterfield believed that all human institutions were under God's judgment, and that this judgment often was most devastating on men and nations that tried to arrogate to themselves the powers and wisdom of Providence. He buttressed this claim with copious references to the course of modern European history and the teachings of the biblical tradition, as well as the insights of the great Greek tragedians, whose works he deeply cherished and whose admonitions against hubris he considered relevant for all ages. In Butterfield's words, judgment "falls heaviest on those who come to think themselves gods, who fly in the face of Providence and history, who put their trust in man-made systems and worship the work of their own hands, and who say that the strength of their own right arm gave them the victory."[24]

Few twentieth-century historians have had as sympathetic an understanding of modern science and its beneficial aspects as Butterfield. As indicated earlier, his 1949 classic, *The Origins of Modern Science*, was a pivotal step in the flowering of the discipline of the history of science; it was the work of a Christian mind embracing modern science, neither slavishly nor reluctantly but acceptingly, with an awareness of the major role it had played in the last three hundred years of Western civilization, a role that Butterfield knew was likely to become even more firmly established in the late twentieth century and beyond. Yet Butterfield also was sensitive to the exaggerated hopes modern man had placed in science and to the idolatrous pretensions in the service of which science was being continually harnessed. For him it was no surprise, therefore, that one of God's severest judgments on twentieth-century man, the development of nuclear weapons, had fallen precisely on the very processes through which man arrogantly had imagined he could establish a permanent utopia on the basis of his own resources. The supposed fountain of eternal progress and human happiness, modern science, had produced a draught so bitter as to throw into doubt the survival of the human race.

The invention of nuclear weapons also illustrated for Butterfield two aspects of judgment in history with which the Greek tragedians and biblical prophets were familiar. First, man was often the executor of his own judgment, and the means whereby he hoped to escape from his limitations turned out in the end to be the ones that frustrated his overreaching designs. The empires of Napoleon and Hitler were destroyed by precisely the same kind of advanced military and political organization and discipline on the part of their adversaries through which both conquerors achieved their early successes. In a similar fashion, nuclear weapons were the fruit of that alliance between the scientific and political establishments on which many Western thinkers from Descartes onwards had posited the solution of mankind's political troubles. The second aspect of judgment, intimately related to the first, was the pervasiveness of its operation. No human being; no form of culture, society or government; no institution, regardless of how laudable were its purposes, was immune to the kind of creeping pretensions of centrality that sooner or later blurred its vision and brought about its fall.

A few years after the end of World War II, Butterfield commented that the great cataclysm which Germany had endured was a judgment on her worship of military might and an uncontrolled urge for greatness.[25] The great Dutch historian Peter Geyl took Butterfield to task for this remark and challenged vigorously the very idea of bringing the notion of judgment into the historian's craft. Butterfield's efforts to think at two different levels, to examine history in the light of purely secular, strictly causal developments while at the same time keeping an eye open for what the hand of God might be doing, were a potential source of intellectual confusions, Geyl charged. How could Butterfield or anyone else, asked Geyl, distinguish the fate of Germany from that of the Baltic countries, which although they did not engage in wars of conquest and actually surrendered peacefully to the Russians in 1940, yet suffered the loss of independence and the deportation of millions to Siberia? Was the notion of judgment of any use to the historian?[26]

Possibly the best reply that could be made to Geyl's criticism is that he missed the subtlety of Butterfield's way of thinking. Only two pages following the controversial statement on Germany's judgment, Butterfield wrote, "if Germany is under judgment so are all of us—the whole of our existing order and the very fabric of our civilisation." And, he added, the judgment which lies in the structure of history gives none of us the right to act as judges over others, or to gloat over the misfortunes of the foreigner, or to scorn our neighbours as people under punishment. There is a sense in which all that we may say on this subject and all the moral verdicts that we may pass on human history are only valid in their application as self-judgments—only useful in so far as we bring them home to ourselves. When we are relating our personalities to the whole drama of human destiny, when we are learning to gain the right feeling for the intimate structure of history, we always come to regions where the most important truths only have an inner reference and an inner ratification—as in the case of falling in love, when only we ourselves know our ultimate feelings, and these are hardly matter for common discourse even if they are capable of communication at all. In the privacy of this room I may say that Germany has come under judgment for what people call her Prussianism or for her adherence to a militaristic tradition. I know, however, that I have no *right* to say any such thing, and I very much doubt whether it would be within the competence of the technical historian to assert it. Here is the kind of truth which is only effective provided it is adopted and taken to heart by the nation concerned, as a matter between itself and God—we as outsiders, and third parties, are not entitled to presume upon it.[27]

The realization that his own endeavors and the institutions he sought to preserve stood under God's judgment and were continually found wanting could provide the statesman with the humility and clarity of vision necessary for good statecraft. And if, as Reinhold Niebuhr wrote, "it is through the judgment of God, who stands against all human pride and pretension, that the inclination of men and nations to make themselves the false center of universal history is broken in principle," then a corporate awareness of divine judgment could temper those passions within the heart of the common man that contribute to national self-righteousness and aggressiveness in foreign policy.[28]

Like Martin Wight, Reinhold Niebuhr, and other contemporary Christian thinkers with whom he was acquainted, Butterfield had a sense of the mysterious, sometimes almost elusive, quality of many of God's judgments. Although all human systems had tainted origins and soiled mechanisms, some were spared their deserved retribution and were allowed to prosper, at times because of the unusual virtue or skill of a few men, at other times thanks to the short-run efficiency of sheer power. There was great truth in the simple words of an old preacher which Butterfield's close friend,

Martin Wight, loved: "Everything you do today, or I do, affects not only what is going to happen but what has already happened, years and centuries ago. Maybe you can't change what has passed, but you can change all the meaning of what has passed. You can even take all the meaning away."[29] Through concrete acts of political forgiveness, moderation, and reconciliation, a statesman could help to avert or postpone the judgment which he and his people deserved for previous violations of the moral law of humanity. A moderate Bismarck seeking to limit Germany's expansion after 1871, a Lyndon Johnson extending full participation in American society to the long-oppressed blacks, a small group of French and German leaders working together in the aftermath of World War II to transform the traditional hostility between their countries into a relationship of mutual security and prosperity are some of the images of political wisdom at work recognizing implicitly or explicitly, what Butterfield called the operation of a moral judgment in the created universe, a recognition followed by creative action.

In keeping with his Christian hope and his devotion to the Rankean search for moral order and constructive possibilities out of the chaos and evil of history, Butterfield could discern the good that can come from God's judgment. The fall of the Roman Empire, the violent break of the thirteen colonies from England, and the German catastrophe of 1945 were not in themselves positive human achievements. Each event was an expression of God's judgment, as well as a failure of man's spiritual, moral, and intellectual capacities to handle a specific set of historical circumstances. Later generations, reflecting on their forefathers' failures and attempting to learn something from them, however, evolved new, more creative patterns of order. The great European culture of the Middle Ages, the unique British conception of empire in the nineteenth and twentieth centuries, and the constructive leadership role provided by Germany in postwar Europe all grew, as Butterfield pointed out, out of a corporate experience of judgment and the ensuing release of fresh forces of spiritual and political regeneration. Thus, the statesman's awareness of judgment could be accompanied by enduring hope in the face of the perpetual chaos of international politics. From Butterfield's Christian perspective, the sore chastisement of judgment, when humbly accepted as the deserved fruit of our moral failures and as a lesson to be learned, leads not to the despair and fatalism of fallen titans, of Napoleons and Hitlers in their last days, but to the serene hope which searches in the midst of the wreckage for whatever opportunities are available to build anew.

III

The Wisdom of Politics

Politics will, to the end of history, be an area where conscience and power meet, where the ethical and coercive factors of human life will interpenetrate and work out their tentative and uneasy compromises.

Reinhold Niebuhr

5

The tragedy of politics and power

For Sir Herbert Butterfield, the political life of man in all its rich variety and knotty complexities presented historians and philosophers with some of their most difficult intellectual dilemmas. From the perspective of either history or philosophy, politics was a problem baffling the most gifted minds and taxing man's moral and intellectual energies to the utmost.

The problematical nature of politics was due, to a considerable extent, to the difficulty of bringing about the degree of peace and order required for the growth of civilization and human reasonableness in a world from which it was impossible to banish disorder, struggle, and chaos permanently. Despite his typically English regard for the possibilities of reason in politics, Butterfield had been sufficiently touched by the tragic events of the twentieth century, the overtones of existentialism implicit in the poetry of Paul Valéry that he loved, and the political realism of his Augustinian theology not to place too much faith in the supposed transformation of politics by reason, which was eagerly expected by many liberals and rationalists during his lifetime. Instead, in *Christianity, Diplomacy and War* and other works Butterfield described man's fundamental political problem, both within the state and in the realm of international relations, as that of building the glasslike, fragile edifice of civilization atop the inherently unstable volcano of human passions, irrationality, and disorder. He chided the twentieth century for forgetting what other ages had learned through great pain and suffering: that the attainment and preservation of order, peace, and civilization require great skill, energy, and creativity and the restraint of the powerful forces of disorder built into human existence.[1] Even in a highly stable political order, such as that formed by the Concert of Powers in nineteenth-century Europe, for example, the volcano continued to rumble underneath the seemingly tranquil surface; the tremors were controlled and widespread chaos kept away through the continued operation of the balance of power, coupled with the exercise of political civility, moderation, and the awareness that all the members of the political order had more to gain by keeping the order functioning than by destroying it.

In Butterfield's insistence on the vulnerability of civilization and the difficulties of achieving limited order in a world of disorder, there is an existentialist theme that resonates through the Old and New Testaments, Augustine, Pascal, and Dostoevsky. In *Notes from Underground*, for instance, Dostoevsky parodied the illusion, not limited to the nineteenth century, of finding with the help of reason and science a simple and permanent solution to the political problem:

> Shower upon man every earthly blessing, drown him in bliss so that nothing but bubbles would dance on the surface of his bliss, as on a sea; give him such economic prosperity that he would have nothing else to do but sleep, eat cakes and busy himself with ensuring the continuation of world history and even then man, out of sheer ingratitude, sheer libel, would play you some loathsome trick. He would even risk his cakes and would deliberately desire the most fatal rubbish, the most uneconomical absurdity, simply to introduce into all this positive rationality his fatal fantastic element. It is just his fantastic dreams, his vulgar folly, that he will desire to retain, simply in order to prove to himself (as though that were so necessary) that men still are men and are not piano keys.[2]

With less dramatic forcefulness but equal sarcasm, Butterfield laughed away the same illusion transposed to the level of international affairs.

The problem of politics was inseparable from and exceedingly complicated by the problem of human nature. Butterfield's view of man was Augustinian. Every individual human being was created in the image of God and, therefore, was possessed of the highest worth and dignity. The historian was at his best when he recognized the world around him as primarily "a world of human relations standing over against nature . . . a universe in which every human being is a separate well of life, a separate source of action, and every human being, so far as mundane things are concerned, has his aspect as an end in himself." Human personalities were "the crowning blossom of creation," each of them being "of eternal moment" and having "a value incommensurate with the value of anything else in the created universe."[3] From this it followed that the purpose of politics, international or otherwise, was to safeguard and encourage the pursuit of the good life, to make it possible for every human being to grow in virtue, wisdom, and grace to the fullest extent permitted by the limitations of the human condition.

Chief among these limitations and an outstanding aspect of human nature was the sinfulness of man. In the best tradition of Christian realism,

Butterfield walked the narrow path between cynicism and nihilism on the one hand and utopianism on the other. His emphasis on the dignity of man was accompanied by the recognition that history "uncovers man's universal sin." The pervasiveness of sin in human nature complicated the problem of politics, making it difficult to fulfill human aspirations for the good life and requiring that in many situations the maintenance of order receive priority over other worthy moral and political ends.[4] Indeed, in a world marred by the disorders and struggles arising from human sinfulness, the maintenance of political order was both a highly challenging task and an indispensable precondition for the pursuit of other values.

Butterfield was especially concerned with four broad manifestations of sin in human nature which he thought had major consequences for man's political life throughout the course of history. These were: sin as cupidity and anxiety; sin as self-righteousness; sin as willfulness and presumptuousness; and sin as neglect of opportunities for doing good. Cupidity was a universal trait infecting man at all levels of his existence; it was erroneous to consider it the monopoly of a single economic class, as Marxism did, or to ascribe it to a few human beings whose elimination or rehabilitation would open the door to a golden political future for mankind. The average individual's desire to improve the conditions of his existence, while responsible for much of his creativity and industriousness, was simultaneously a source of political friction and struggle whenever he pursued it as he often did without a proper concern for the betterment of others in his society or the welfare of other nations in the international community. Perceptively, Butterfield argued that the search for the causes of international conflict should focus less on the extraordinarily criminal man—a Hitler or a Mussolini—and more on the millions of ordinary, decent citizens everywhere whose eagerness to advance up the economic and social ladder and to see their nation attain levels of greatness and power denied to them in their personal lives makes it difficult for any government to follow a foreign policy of soberness, limited aspirations, and reasonable diplomacy. Much of the fault for international tensions lies with "the mediocre desires, the intellectual confusions and the willful moods of the average man, the man in the street. The real trouble is the moderate cupidity of Everyman—his ordinary longing to advance a little further than his father, or simply to increase his sales—even just his dread of a decline in his standard of living. This, when multiplied by millions, can build up into a tremendous pressure on government."[5]

The "Everyman" whom both modern democracy and communism worship, but whose fallenness Butterfield was prophetically unafraid to underline, was also a self-righteous creature. He generally believed that virtue and service to progress were the prerogatives of his country, while warmongering and unreasonableness were those of its adversaries, this belief being a derivation of the personal self-righteousness and moral superiority that most individuals feel towards their fellow human beings even within the same political community. The roots of political self-righteousness in human nature were well described by the noted French philosopher Blaise Pascal when he wrote:

> The nature of self-love and of this human Ego is to love self only and consider self only. But what will man do? He cannot prevent this object that he loves from being full of faults and wants. . . . He wants to be the object of love and esteem among men, and he sees that his faults merit only their hatred and contempt. This embarrassment in which he finds himself produces in him the most unrighteous and criminal passion that can be imagined; for he conceives a mortal enmity against that truth which reproves him, and which convinces him of his faults. He would annihilate it, but unable to destroy it in its essence, he destroys it as far as possible in his own knowledge and in that of others; that is to say, he devotes all his attention to hiding his faults both from others and from himself, and he cannot endure either that others should point them out to him, or that they should see them.[6]

For Butterfield this form of self-righteousness, when transposed within the consciousness of the average citizen to the level of international relations so as to enable him to identify himself with his morally superior nation, had a collective political impact as harmful as that of cupidity.

There was another dimension of self-righteousness with which Butterfield was concerned: self-righteousness on the part of political leaders. Men who exercised power were highly vulnerable to this form of sin, and ironically the higher the statesman's moral idealism the more likely he was to claim moral sanctity for his politics and decry the alleged immorality of those who opposed him. Men who claimed to be the bearers of absolute morality in politics, a Woodrow Wilson or a Gladstone, fell prey to self-righteousness more readily than those statesmen, such as Churchill and Richelieu, whose regard for the moral law was accompanied by the knowledge that their own hands and purposes were inevitably soiled in the rough-and-tumble of the political world. Whether in its collective or individual manifestations, self-righteousness was for Butterfield one of the worst sins politically, the "one sin that locks people up in all their other sins," fastening "men and nations more tightly than ever in their predicaments." Whereas the human condition cried out for reconciliation, self-righteousness produced the opposite result, men being frequently "goaded to greater wickedness by the exasperating conduct of the stiffnecked."[7]

The combination of self-righteousness and utopianism peculiar to the foreign policies of many twentieth-century democracies was one against which Butterfield warned, as he described the destructive process set in motion by political visionaries whose projects for world harmony foundered on the rock of man's universal cupidity. When his projects went awry, the disillusioned idealist quickly found culprits with a vengeance, bringing "from under his sleeve that doctrine of human sinfulness which it would have been so much better for him to have faced fairly and squarely in the first instance." In the utopian mind, "the sinners are fewer in number but they are diabolically wicked in order to make up for it."[8] The utopian statesman came to see history as a mighty battle between the forces of good, which he represented, and those of evil, against which he supposedly struggled. In the end he became absorbed in his own self-righteousness, incapable of perceiving his limitations or forgiving those of others and unwittingly contributing through his stiffening willfulness to the deadlocks at the root of political conflict.

"If there were no more willfulness throughout the whole of human nature than exists in this room at the present moment," Butterfield once said, "it would be sufficient to tie events into knots and to produce those deadlocks which all of us know in our little world, while on the scale of the nation-state it would be enough, with its complexities, ramifications and congealings, to bring about the greatest war in history."[9] Willfulness and presumptuousness were the consequences of self-righteousness, simple pride, and that burning desire to master the course of history which Butterfield castigated so harshly throughout his commentaries on Providence and divine judgment. He aptly summed up his view of the matter when he wrote that most wars fought by man since his earliest recorded beginnings had been struggles between "one half-right that was too willful and one half-right that was too proud."[10] As these words show, Butterfield's belief in the universality of sin left little room for political Manicheanisms of any sort.

Another manifestation of sin in human nature which Butterfield considered highly relevant to political life was sin as omission, as the neglect of opportunities for doing good. The words from the general confession in the Anglican Book of Common Prayer, "we have left undone those things which we ought to have done," held great meaning for Butterfield. They conveyed the unpleasant but necessary truth that sins of omission were often more frequent and destructive than those of commission, and he was opposed to any attempts at modernizing the language of the confession that might have blunted the theological forcefulness of these words. He agreed with his friend Martin Wight, who wrote that, "we are not well-meaning peoples doing our best; we are miserable sinners, living under judgment . . . well-meaning like Pilate, every day crucifying Christ afresh."[11] The sin of Pilate, like that of many a decent citizen or statesman, was one of omission, of not exploiting to the full the moral opportunities available to him by virtue of the power at his disposal.

In conversations with friends, Butterfield often referred to World War I as a great catastrophe brought about largely through minor sins of omission on the part of many people rather than the deliberate acts of a few evildoers. It was not only "the mediocre desires, the intellectual confusions and the willful moods," but also the sins of omission of leaders such as the Kaiser, the Czar, Sir Edward Grey, Emperor Franz Joseph, and others that gradually led to a political impasse and the unleashing of a disastrous war that none of them really wanted. A marginally stronger exertion towards accommodation, a more vigorous effort to reduce tensions and fear, or a slightly broader definition of the national interest by any of these statesmen might have averted the great tragedy. Thus, remarked Butterfield, "a civilization may be wrecked without any spectacular crimes or criminals but by constant petty breaches of faith and minor complicities on the part of men generally considered very nice people." [12] The greater the power available to a statesman, the wider are the ramifications of his sins of omission.

Cupidity, self-righteousness, willfulness, and sloth in doing good are all variants of that inordinate love of self which Christian theology traditionally has recognized as the quintessence of sin. Augustine, for example, drew the contrast between the City of God, ruled by the love of God, and the City of Man, whose dominant passions were the love of self and contempt for God. Blaise Pascal, after pointing out that "the propensity to self is the beginning of all disorder in war, in politics, in economy," complained about the "perverted judgment that makes every one place himself above the rest of the world, and prefer his own good, and the continuance of his own good fortune and life, to that of the rest of the world." [13] In the tradition of Augustine and Pascal, Butterfield reminded his contemporaries of the pervasiveness in political life of the love of self, arguing that any moral examination must begin with oneself and one's nation rather than the adversary of the moment, on whom we are tempted to place the blame for the moral failures of international relations.

If human nature complicated any attempts at understanding or mastering international politics, so did the problem of power. Through his debate with Sir Lewis Namier and his followers, Butterfield revealed that he saw politics as much more than a chaotic Thrasymachean struggle in which might made right and the quest for power was the dominant theme. The search for the common good and the reasoned elaboration and implementation of moral purposes also played a major role in Butterfield's conception of politics. The political philosophy embedded in his writings can be described as the herculean effort of a highly catholic mind to keep in simultaneous perspective, in a never-ending and sometimes playful tension, these two dimensions of politics: politics as man's quest for the highest practicable good and politics as the struggle for power. For Butterfield, both dimensions were mutually supportive of each other and intimately connected with one another. No political cause, however noble, could succeed without the use and understanding of power; no quest for power, however unscrupulous, could achieve lasting results without at least a tacit appeal to moral justification.[14]

Butterfield's understanding of power and its central place in man's political life is illuminated by his relationship to the historical school of Friedrich Meinecke (1862–1954), the eminent German historian with whom Butterfield felt a special intellectual kinship. Throughout his long and prolific life, Meinecke had a consuming interest in the relationship of power to politics and the relationship of both of these to morality. Inspired by Ranke's exalted vision of the role of power in man's political life, yet deeply shaken by Germany's defeat in World War I and the doubts this defeat threw on the soundness of the ideology of power politics that had ruled Wilhelmine Germany, Meinecke wrote *Machiavellism: The Doctrine of Raison d'État and Its Place in Modern History* in 1925. It was a historical and philosophical study of the concept of reason of state from Machiavelli to Ranke and Treitschke, and it served Meinecke as a means to explore the political and ethical pitfalls and virtues involved in the statesman's exercise of power. The work had a profound influence on Butterfield, who used it as a foundation for his own thinking on the subject; numerous references to it and excerpts from it can be found in Butterfield's notes for the unfinished *History of Diplomacy* and his 1975 Martin Wight memorial lecture on raison d'état.[15]

Like Meinecke, Butterfield understood the morally ambiguous role which the exercise of power played in politics. In his numerous writings on the balance of power, for example, Butterfield drew attention to the dangers that faced a state-system whenever it was unable to check the expansion of power of one of its members. In such perilous circumstances, power had both destructive and constructive dimensions; it was destructive whenever the one-sided expansion was allowed to proceed unmolested but constructive whenever power was built up and distributed so as to bring about an equilibrium and deter the expansionist ambitions of any single state or group of states. Similar moral ambiguities colored the behavior of the Great Powers in the international system. While the Great Powers of nineteenth-century Europe were not above the practice of using their weaker neighbors as pawns in their quest for greatness, they also frequently performed a moral function by using their tremendous power to maintain order and stability. Even the institutions of international law were not free from the moral ambiguities of power. Insofar as international law aided the processes of diplomacy and strengthened the operation of what Butterfield called "the ethical factor in international relations," it played a decidedly moral role. But Butterfield was also acutely conscious of the marriage of convenience of international law and legitimacy to power and of the ease with which an international legal regime became a means by which powerful states maintained an advantageous status quo at the expense of the weak.[16]

In general, however, Butterfield tended to pay more attention to the morally and politically destructive features of power than to the positive ones, the former being perhaps much more challenging to manage and more frequently found than the latter. Without going as far as the Swiss historian Jacob Burckhardt, whose condemnation of power politics failed to take into account that the exercise of power was necessary to mitigate the abuses of power, Butterfield retained throughout his life an Actonian suspiciousness towards power in men and nations. Interestingly, however, this suspiciousness did not lead him to an abhorrence of and flight from all power politics, as was and is the case with many liberals and Christian dissenters. Instead, this suspiciousness was the starting point for an inquiry into how power could be used to manage power and how power politics, when understood and handled in the full light of their troublesome reality, could be the means for establishing limited order and the political foundation for broader moral purposes.

For Butterfield, one of the cardinal axioms of politics was the thesis put forward by Lord Acton towards the close of the first of his *Lectures on Modern History* concerning "the tendency of power as such to expand indefinitely, transcending all barriers at home and abroad, until it is met by a force superior to it."[17] The control and management of such expansion was among the foremost problems any political order, domestic or international, constantly faced. The root of the problem was human cupidity and the anxiety it generated. In a world of grasping human beings, ever greater power was necessary, not only to augment one's security and prosperity but also to prevent one's own power from being gradually eroded by that of others. As Thomas Hobbes put it in his *Leviathan*, in words whose historical and political significance Butterfield appreciated deeply,

> The nature of Power, is in this point, like to Fame, increasing as it proceeds; or like the motion of heavy bodies, which the further they go, make still the more hast. . . . So that in the first place, I put for a generall inclination of all mankind, a perpetuall and restlesse desire of Power after power, that ceaseth onely in Death. And the cause of this, is not alwayes that a man hopes for a more intensive delight, than he has already attained to; or that he cannot be content with a moderate power: but because he cannot assure the

power and means to live well, which he hath present, without the acquisition of more.[18]

Butterfield saw international conflict in some of its most intense forms, such as World War I or the Soviet-American cold war, as a tragic predicament, one side of it being the cupidity and Hobbesian lust for power propelling a state's foreign policy, the other side a pervasive fear resulting from the awareness that other states had similar desires for power, material goods, and national glory.[19] A vicious, tragic cycle ensued. A state's efforts to augment its security could not but alarm its rivals who knew that such security was easily translatable into aggressive power. Their reaction, reasonable as it seemed to them, was interpreted by the other state as further proof that it had to intensify its quest for strength if it were to survive. Thus, even the best-intentioned and most peace-loving statesmen could be drawn, however incongruously in relation to their avowed moral purposes, into the same suspiciousness and immoderate desire for power of which they accused others. This was the tragic, almost intractable dilemma into which international politics could become knotted. As Butterfield described it:

> There could be a United States and a Russia standing at the top of the world, exactly equal in power, exactly equal in virtue; and each could fear with some justice that the other might steal a march on it, neither of them understanding for a moment—neither of them even crediting—the counterfear of the other. Each could be sure of its own good intentions, but might not trust the other, since one can never really pierce to the interior of anybody else. Mutual resentment would come to be doubled because, on the top of everything, each party felt that the other was withholding just the thing that would enable it to feel secure. This situation may never exist in its purity, but the essential predicament underlies international relations generally, making even simple problems sometimes insoluble.[20]

Two broad responses to the tragedy of power politics were available to the realist statesman unwilling to surrender to the captivating charms of utopianism. One was nihilism, the belief that the struggle for power requires the subordination to it of all normative standards whenever necessary. The individualistic atomistic philosophy at the heart of nihilism also implies that in international politics there is an insufficient basis for the existence of common interests among states and therefore diplomacy has to be conducted as if the course of international relations is generally a zero-sum game. Nihilism thus downplays both the validity and usefulness of normative standards, as well as the possibilities for sociability, accommodation, and cooperation among states. It is the model of political reality associated with Hobbes and Machiavelli.

Butterfield thought that, while international politics exhibited many of the features that Hobbes and Machiavelli so perceptively had discerned, their observations were nevertheless incomplete. Butterfield had a lifelong fascination with Machiavelli; the Florentine's devotion to historical study as a source of political wisdom and his Faustian wrestlings with the problem of morality in politics intrigued the tranquil Cambridge don. Unlike many Machiavelli critics such as Leo Strauss or Friedrich Meinecke, Butterfield was hesitant to condemn Machiavelli as an evil genius through whom, in Meinecke's words, "the devil forced his way into the Kingdom of God."[21] But, even after giving Machiavelli ample credit for the judiciousness and soundness of many of his political teachings, Butterfield did not hesitate to criticize him on three general counts.[22]

First, Machiavelli was too rigid and selective in his reading of history; he was too eager to discover in past events confirmation for his political philosophy and not sufficiently attuned to the subtle convolutions through which change occurs in the historical process—Machiavelli's view of historical causation was too narrow for Butterfield.[23] Second, Machiavelli's eagerness to transform statecraft and historical interpretation into hard sciences led him to an error which Butterfield considered typical of the professorial mind at work in politics, the supplanting of flexible political prudence by supposedly universal canons of political wisdom which in reality failed to do justice to the diversity and richness of political life. Hence, Machiavelli—and Butterfield borrowed this criticism from Machiavelli's great contemporary, Guicciardini—focused on the conduct of politics in highly unsettled times and conditions of extraordinary turmoil and violence, but had little advice for the statesman living in a political setting of relative stability. The prince addressed by Machiavelli was an adventurer who had to work hard to keep his newly acquired throne. While Napoleon, Lenin, Mussolini, and Hitler could model themselves on this prince with varied degrees of success as their reward, the practical statesmen of well-established societies—Bismarck, Churchill, or Kissinger—had to go elsewhere to complete their political education. Machiavelli's emphasis on the usefulness of the clever ruse, the devious strategem, or the act of unspeakable ruthlessness and violence was not only that of a detached intellectual who personally would have hesitated to resort to these things; it was also a one-sided perspective that failed to take into consideration the role that normative standards, the hammering out of genuine common interests, and the pursuit of cooperative—as distinct from confrontational—behavior play in everyday political life. The lonely Machiavellian statesman, like the self-reliant Machiavellian state, was unrealistically autonomous from the community of moral purposes and common political interests through which man introduces a measure of harmony and coherence into politics. Butterfield did not hesitate to point out that, for all his fame as a theorist, Machiavelli was a signal failure as a politician and diplomat.

Finally, Butterfield considered politically and morally unacceptable Machiavelli's general thesis in *The Prince* that

> how we live is so different from how we ought to live that he who studies what ought to be done rather than what is done will learn the way to his downfall rather than to his preservation. A man striving in every way to be good will meet his ruin among the great number who are not good. Hence it is necessary for a prince, if he wishes to remain in power, to learn how not to be good and to use his knowledge or refrain from using it as he may need.[24]

Butterfield commented:

> A man can scarcely be accused of any great immorality if he accepts the standards of his time and consents to live as the world lives. The thesis might prove, however, more pointed and more dangerous if it implied that men should take as their standard of conduct the morality of their day conceived at its worst; and it is important to note in this respect that Machiavelli had a remarkably low view of human nature. He does not recommend us to break a treaty merely when we think that the other party is going to break it; he says that since men are wicked the other party may always be presumed to be about to break it. . . .
>
>   . . . in Machiavelli the doctrine "live as the world lives" is the ordinary vulgar doctrine that morality does not pay; its only purport is the reduction of the conduct of good men to the standards of that of the worst, and it is difficult to see how an invitation to immorality could have been expressed in other terms or placed on a more comprehensive basis.[25]

A different realist response to the tragedy of power politics was that represented by one of Butterfield's favorite historical personages, Cardinal Richelieu. Like Machiavelli, the great French statesman has been easily maligned as a ruthless cynic by historians of lesser subtlety than Butterfield. But the founder of the modern French state offered to Butterfield a paradigm of political wisdom and realism more balanced, more comprehensive, and generally more useful to the practical statesman than that of the Florentine genius.[26]

Richelieu drew a much sharper distinction than Machiavelli between the ruler's welfare and that of the political community over which he reigned. Whenever the two clashed, the welfare of the community was to take precedence over that of the ruler or any other private citizen. Richelieu became prince minister at a time of rampant civil strife and political disorder, when the king himself and groups such as the nobility and the Huguenots wielded their vast power with greater regard for their private social or religious interests than the interests of France. Believing that the French state, as guardian of the political community of France, had a moral responsibility to fulfill in maintaining public order and subordinating the interests of the parts to that of the whole, Richelieu developed the doctrine of raison d'état, or reason of state. The state had a reason of its own, a justification grounded in its moral and political purposes, which transcended and took primacy over the fragmentary reasons, the disparate interests, of smaller groups and individuals within society.

For Butterfield, Richelieu's ethical achievements in politics were numerous and significant. The doctrine of reason of state, by subordinating the king to the state and by connecting the state's purposes with the maintenance of civil order and the advancement of the welfare and security of the entire community, represented a creative breakthrough for moral considerations into the course of politics. While later imitators of Richelieu in France and elsewhere often turned reason of state into a monstrous political Baal whose invocation sufficed to justify any crimes, Butterfield thought that Richelieu himself had avoided the slippery descent into nihilism by defining reason of state within the bounds of what was both reasonable and morally right. Richelieu preserved another vital link between morality and reason of state when he wrote that, in political matters involving difficult moral choices, a statesman should seek the opinions of theologians and doctors of the Church. This was the voice of a man unwilling to jettison the anchor of transcendence yet aware that the precarious relationship of morality to politics could not be dictated by a simple science of statecraft, as Machiavelli or some of his religious opponents would have suggested, but instead had to be forged within the conscience of the statesman through much agony and searching, in fear and trembling.

Richelieu was also much more conscious than Machiavelli of the existence in international relations of a "reason of system" within which the individual reasons of states had to function. France's raison d'état required the maintenance of a balance of power in the wider European system of states where she existed. And to the extent that she had to be concerned about such balance, France had to resort to diplomacy and to the strengthening of common political interests with other states instead of remaining in suspicious aloofness from and unremitting hostility toward all other states. Thus, international politics for Richelieu was not a zero-sum game, and sociability among states was a reality forced upon even the most independent-minded rulers by the existence of other political units with which it was necessary to deal continuously. Richelieu himself demonstrated the validity of these observations when, in the course of the Thirty Years' War, he allied France with the Protestant powers so as to prevent the Catholic Habsburgs from upsetting the balance of power in Central Europe and thereby threatening France's independence.

Sociability among states also implied some respect for the moral law. One of the features of Richelieu's statecraft that Butterfield appreciated most was the connection which the French master of realpolitik drew between the observance of morality and the requirements of diplomacy, as in this passage from Richelieu's *Political Testament*:

> Kings should be very careful with regard to the treaties they conclude, but having concluded them they should observe them religiously. I well know that many statesmen advise to the contrary, but without considering here what the Christian religion offers in answer to such advice, I maintain that the loss of honor is worse than the loss of life itself. A great prince should sooner put in jeopardy both his own interests and even those of the state than break his word, which he can never violate without losing his reputation and by consequence the greatest instrument of sovereigns. [27]

This was a far cry from Machiavelli's suggestions that morality did not pay and that only rarely could a prince's best interests be served effectively by ethical behavior on his part.

Richelieu, according to Butterfield, combined an understanding of power politics with the sense of moral responsibility that ought to accompany the exercise of power. Moreover, while Machiavelli and Hobbes had envisioned the interplay of all political relationships in the domestic and international scene as a choice between either tyranny and absolute hegemony or the anarchic pursuit by individual participants of their self-interest in bitter conflict among themselves, Richelieu thought that, at least in the field of international relations, a third alternative was feasible. Through the policies of the balance of power and diplomacy, statesmen could search for and often discover means of reconciling the divergent interests of their respective states; imperial hegemony or unlimited international anarchy were not the only avenues open to international statesmanship. And, insofar as diplomacy played a key role in promoting and bringing about the accommodation of widely disparate national interests, it served a moral purpose in international politics. Richelieu's awareness of this moral dimension of diplomacy was for Butterfield one of his outstanding political and ethical achievements. [28] In the cardinal's statecraft Butterfield thought the student of international relations could find a paradigm of greater political realism and ethical integrity than those of the pure Machiavellians or the utopian liberals with their Manichean self-righteousness and pretensions to transcending permanently the tragedy of international politics.

For Butterfield, power, despite the grave pitfalls connected with its exercise, was indispensable and invaluable in the moral task of bringing about order in international politics. Thus, while Butterfield was intensely aware of the corrupting influence of power, he, unlike Acton, also had an appreciative eye for the contribution to international order and stability that could be made by great powers and their leaders. Otto von Bismarck and Henry Kissinger were admirable because they combined a keen, Machiavellian understanding of power politics with an awareness of their moral obligation to wield their state's power responsibly in support of international order. Often it was the hard-boiled realists like Bismarck, Kissinger, and Churchill, men who had no utopian illusions and who knew the workings of power politics intimately well, who left behind the most lasting achievements in international order and accommodation.[29]

Butterfield took far more seriously than most Christians the admonition of Jesus to "give to Caesar what is Caesar's, and to God what is God's." He interpreted these words in the light of Augustine's distinction between the City of Man and the City of God, the former realm having a logic and a modus operandi of its own which had to be studied and observed by those charged with the responsibility of promoting earthly order and peace. Thus, even a Christian statesman whose ultimate loyalties lay in the City of God would be misguided and would cause great harm to those under his care, in adopting the logic and methods of the heavenly city for conducting the affairs of the earthly one. Obviously, the Christian statesman's transcendent loyalties could still illumine his earthly work, but the light could be partial and refracted at best. He could refrain from lying, cheating, and poisoning his enemies, as Richelieu had advised; but to bring about an amelioration of international conflict he was most likely to reach his objectives if he relied on a balance of power and hard-headed diplomacy instead of the hoped-for fulfillment of the Kingdom of God on earth.

For Butterfield, as for Clausewitz, power, even when guided by and strictly subject to higher ends, had its own grammar, the rules of which could not be violated with impunity. A Christian statesman might be determined to exercise his country's military power responsibly; he might go to great lengths to ensure that no war was entered into except under the most pressing circumstances, after an enemy aggressor took the first step and placed his people under the threat of total annihilation. Yet even such a Christian statesman could not be oblivious to the grammar of power. In peacetime he had to maintain an adequate military establishment stocked with weapons of terrifying destructiveness. And once he was forced into war he had to send thousands of men to their deaths and take responsibility for acts that in his personal life he would never commit.[30]

Similarly, as Butterfield was reminded by Augustine, a Christian judge, no matter how just and merciful, faced situations in which he had to punish a man with death or the forfeiture of his liberty and goods, even though that same judge in his private life might turn his cheek to a robber and suffer violence upon himself rather than strike back in self-defense. The exercise of power in international or domestic affairs followed a grammar far different from that of love. It was a grammar of coercion, limited violence, and force made necessary by the tragic fallenness permeating the human condition.[31]

For Butterfield this meant that there was no way for the statesman to avoid soiled hands even when he was exercising power on behalf of morally good ends. The City of Man was constituted in such a way that even worthy political ends required means that were not totally pure. A statesman pursuing peace and the lessening of international tensions might have to deal with tyrannical regimes, look the other way when valuable allies committed moral wrongs, and use as bargaining chips in diplomacy subtle threats and oblique allusions to his state's might and wealth. For self-righteous politicians in power, this was a truth too bitter to swallow. They tried to square the circle in public, describing as virtuous and pure acts that, if committed by their foreign adversaries or domestic opponents, they would quickly label immoral. But, for Butterfield, knowledge of the inescapability of soiled hands in politics could be therapeutic. It could be a guard against self-delusion and self-righteousness, an inspiration to humility and, in the case of the Christian statesman, a powerful prodding to continuous repentance and to the quest for forgiveness at the feet of the crucified Christ.

A powerful man, be it a philanthropist or a secretary of state, might claim the most thorough virtue for all the means he employed in securing admittedly good ends. But he was not likely to see how much of his success was due to either the fear his power inspired or the desire to please him so as to benefit eventually from his good favors. Such a powerful man would move about unaware of the long shadow cast by his great power, a shadow that affected the way others dealt with him. As with a powerful state, a powerful man did not need to flaunt his power openly; he did not need to resort to direct coercion or open violence. All that was necessary for him to have his way was that others be aware of his power; and this awareness could be so quiet and unobtrusive as to give rise to the illusion that it was the man's virtue or intelligence, rather than his power, that caused him to be treated with such deference. Whether one had in mind a powerful individual or the collectivity encompassed by a powerful state, the great shadow cast by power obscured the power holder's vision of himself or itself, heightening the tendency to see virtue in one's actions when there was none and diminishing the opportunities for a realistic self-examination.[32] This was another reason why the shadow of power and the means that accompany the exercise of power were not clean and could never be so, even though relative distinctions could and should be made about degrees of ethical integrity. Butterfield had the rare courage to contemplate this sad dimension of power, this perpetual ambiguity if not outright uncleanness involved in the use of power even for worthy ends. His was the valor of a man willing to see the tragedy of politics and power in its full ramifications. It required equal courage and creativity to reflect, as he also did, on the means by which a statesman, despite the moral and political obstacles standing in his way, could perform the moral task of bringing a measure of peace and order to international relations.

6

Statesmanship as the search
for order

In his thinking on international politics, Herbert Butterfield paid close attention to three key institutions through which a semblance of order and harmony could be brought to the chaotic course of world affairs: the balance of power, diplomacy, and an international order. He was quick to grasp the significance for international relations of Lord Acton's dictum, "power tends to corrupt and absolute power corrupts absolutely." No matter how virtuous a state and its leaders may be, the acquisition of great power by that state will have a corrupting effect on its foreign policy, for it will discover that it can act with impunity. Such was the case of Phillip II's Spain, Louis XIV's France, and post-Bismarckian Germany. The Actonian insights as applied by Butterfield to international politics thus supplied him with a powerful philosophical justification for the policies of the balance of power.[1]

Butterfield was most concerned with the balance of power as an equilibrium of forces which statesmen deliberately will contrive in order to keep any state from gaining supremacy over the rest. As a carefully calculated policy disentangled from ideological factors and aimed at the manipulation of power, the balance of power attained its most refined theoretical articulation in the late seventeenth century and throughout the eighteenth century. Even Machiavelli, whose political sagacity Butterfield admired in many respects, lacked a coherent understanding of the balance of power. His hesitant gropings with the issue yielded little more than the observation that, in a quarrel between two neighboring powers, a state should avoid neutrality and support the one most likely to win; although it is possible that the winner may be ungrateful for such aid, said Machiavelli, this usually will not be the case. Missing in the Florentine's analysis was any reference to the overall equilibrium of forces in a state-system. A statesman deliberately upholding such equilibrium as the best check against rapacious powers might opt for neutrality or even support the weak against the strong as Great Britain did during the Napoleonic Wars lest the strong crush the independence of all. Another flaw perceived by Butterfield in the Machiavellian reflections lay in the illusion, so antithetical to the tenor of Machiavelli's own political thought, that the victor's gratitude would keep it in a friendly disposition towards the powers that helped it.[2]

One of the remarkable characteristics of the balance of power from Butterfield's viewpoint was that its effectiveness did not depend on such unreliable human attributes as gratitude, loyalty, or moral obligation. Whether in the Italy of Lorenzo de' Medici or eighteenth-century Europe, the balance of power was best maintained when all states watched each other with unremitting jealousy, ready at any moment to form new alliances and correct any growing disparities in the distribution of forces. If, as Butterfield said in *Christianity and History*, political institutions should not rely heavily on human goodness, then the balance of power was fit for this fallen world by relying for its propelling motives on human self-interest and for its instrument on force or the threat of it. Although Butterfield referred to the balance of power as a state of affairs brought about through human action, he did not consider it a mere option; a statesman had no choice but to aim towards a balance of power if he was truly alive to his state's long-range interests.[3] Thus, Butterfield's understanding of the balance of power incorporated the twin elements of human purposiveness and determinism which have troubled so many other theorists.

The earlier theorists of the balance of power in modern European history had envisaged the balance in the simple form of a pair of scales, in much the same way that many American policymakers between 1945 and 1970 considered the framework of international politics to be the bipolar balance of power between the Soviet bloc and the Western alliance. Butterfield reckoned it a great advance when, around the late seventeenth century, thinkers such as Fénelon began to put forward a more sophisticated view of the balance of power as a constantly shifting equilibrium among many centers of gravity. In this conception of the balance, "the equilibrium was seen as distributed throughout the whole system, the various states poised against one another like the heavenly bodies in the Newtonian universe—any substantial change in the mass of one of them requiring a possible regrouping of the rest if the balance were to be maintained."[4] This revised image was the product of a growing awareness among Europeans that their states belonged to a common system of political, economic, and military relations; an increase or diminution in the power of any state was likely to be of grave concern to everyone else, requiring a realignment of power away from the stronger state and towards each other.

According to Butterfield, the connection drawn by Fénelon and others between the existence of a European society of states and the maintenance of a general equilibrium implied an abhorrence of ideological wars and of any wars fought for other than limited practical objectives, since they tended to make political compromise difficult and to cause uncontrollable changes in the balance of power. The major consequences of the new European outlook represented by Fénelon were a greater degree of moderation in the conduct of foreign policy—wars were considered temporary quarrels among friends who belonged to the same "club"—and the further development of diplomacy as a fine instrument for the constant measurement and regulation of any shifts in power so as to preserve the overall equilibrium. As Butterfield explained, the eighteenth-century theory of the balance of power

> noted the limits to which a state could safely go either in egotism or altruism and insisted that the diplomat can never afford to ignore the distribution of power, that indeed the virtuous conduct of states might depend on this. And the pattern of the system became printed on the minds of practising diplomats—reinforcing the tendency to constant vigilance and perpetual negotiation—reinforcing also the need for farsightedness, because, once the predominance of a state is a *fait accompli*, the situation is liable to be irreversible.[5]

Diplomacy, the handmaid of the balance of power, gave the statesman another means of attenuating some of the harshest features of international politics. As with the balance of power, the usefulness of diplomacy lay in its suitability to a fallen world in which interests rather than sentiments often dictated a state's foreign policy and power rather than morality defined the limits to state conduct. Behind the facade of proprieties characteristic of diplomacy, the struggle of human wills went on and the outcome of diplomacy was not divorced from the amount of power available to its participants. In other words, diplomacy was not, as some people imagined, an academic discussion in which reason and rightness always prevailed; it was instead a method for carrying out the Hobbesian quest for power in a setting other than the battlefield. Diplomacy, wrote Butterfield,

> is not by any means an achieved Utopia. . . . it is simply the opening of a route by which mankind may gradually progress out of the conditions of the jungle. Men under this system make their decisions after doing a piece of mental arithmetic—after making a calculation of forces and changes—instead of enacting the full tale of violence, with the forces actually colliding and everything really consigned to the hazards of war.[6]

In the process of acting as a substitute for the use of force, diplomacy softened the Hobbesian struggle by introducing into it a degree of reasonableness and a series of factors which, despite their elusiveness, could make the difference between civilization and barbarism. In this respect, diplomacy was "a victory of the human intelligence in its perennial conflict with force and chance," since

> new and more subtle aspects of power—other things besides sheer military strength—are apt to enter into the calculations when the tug-of-war is merely a diplomatic one. A state may even possess what is tantamount to "a pull in negotiation" because, though it is weak in itself, it holds other bargaining counters, and commands other forms of influence or inducement. Alternatively, . . . subtle substitutes or oblique equivalents for force can be brought into play, such as arguments of convenience, appeals to past friendship or attempts to flatter an individual statesman. Force . . . may find its effects diluted when far-sighted statesmanship, or a reputation for reliability, is a factor in the negotiation. And perhaps it is more the case in diplomacy than in war that cleverness in tactics and wisdom in strategy are able to measure themselves against the efficacy of mere power and might. . . . power may not be annulled or cancelled, therefore; but it can be considerably qualified or diluted in the transpositions that take place.[7]

The relationship between diplomacy and force was, therefore, rich with counterpoint. On the one hand the results of diplomacy were closely connected with the will and military capabilities of its participants. Yet, in moving the Hobbesian game from the battlefield to the negotiating table, diplomacy also reduced the role of force and amplified that of the other factors enumerated by Butterfield, thereby civilizing international relations without necessarily transforming their character totally.

It was this adaptability to power politics, combined with its civilizing influence, that made diplomacy such an attractive political mechanism for Butterfield. Its links to power, its gradual approach, and its connection with the true interests of states made diplomacy a more effective even if less spectacular means of introducing a moral element into the course of international relations than the grandiose schemes for transforming world politics overnight put forward recurrently by utopians of all stripes. Whenever it helped to bring about the accommodation of divergent national interests, diplomacy served the moral goal of peace, as it also did whenever it made the conduct of foreign policy less subject to actual resort to force. Moreover, by rewarding the reliability, honesty, and skills of reconciliation of particular negotiators, diplomacy increased the occasions in which morality, reasonableness, and moderation paid political and other rewards in international relations. In both its ends and means, therefore, diplomacy could serve limited yet nonetheless valuable moral purposes. By inducing statesmen to reflect on and measure the long range of their nations' interests, diplomacy sometimes could reveal surprising opportunities to blend political interests with moral objectives, opportunities which statesmen might have missed had they not been involved in the slow, detailed, and intense search for common interests that is at the core of diplomacy.

Butterfield knew that his high regard for the usefulness of classical diplomacy was out of favor with much of the prevailing thought in his lifetime. Punctured by bitter "Wars for Righteousness" and deep ideological hatreds and dominated by the political antics of revolutionary utopians and liberal democrats, all of whom shared an impatience with and contempt for the gradual processes of diplomacy, the twentieth century tried first to transform diplomacy, then to ignore it. Despite its intellectual disrepute, however, diplomacy survived, even if not in its former grandeur and refinement. At the discussions of the British Committee on International Theory, with which Butterfield was closely associated, recurrent themes were the continuing vigor of diplomacy at all levels of the international system and the possibilities for the full restoration of diplomacy to its civilizing and moderating role.[8]

Butterfield agreed with the classical theorists of diplomacy that the duties of the practicing diplomat required that he do more than collect information and assist in the settlement of disputes, invaluable though these were. The diplomat also was "to keep perpetual contact with a foreign country, to build up the reputation of his own nation, and, most of all, to generate confidence."[9] Through constant interaction with society and the government to which he was accredited, the diplomat could help his host country to gain a clear, perhaps even sympathetic, understanding of his own nation's position on numerous foreign policy issues; at the same time, such a diplomat might acquire an accurate understanding of the host country's foreign policy, which he could convey to his superiors at home. Depending on his abilities, and on the extent to which his government made use of him, a professional diplomat could provide much of the badly needed oil in the machinery of international relations, helping to lessen anxieties and the likelihood for misunderstanding. While it was difficult for governments to develop a sympathetic imagination towards their foreign rivals, it was possible, through the diplomat's work, to have such a clear image of the rival's position and capabilities and to convey to him an equally clear picture of one's own, so as to avoid any false steps or overreaching moves by either side.

Because of the enormous potential value of diplomacy to states, Butterfield thought that it should be as major and continuous a resource of foreign policy as armies or economic strategies. Among his favorite passages from Richelieu's *Political Testament* were those in which the cardinal argued that

> it is absolutely necessary to the well-being of the state to negotiate ceaselessly, either openly or secretly, and in all places, even in those from which no present fruits are reaped and still more in those for which no future prospects as yet seem likely. . . . He who negotiates continuously will finally find the right instant to attain his ends, and even if this does not come about, at least it can be said he has lost nothing while keeping abreast of events in the world, which is not of little consequence in the lives of states. Negotiations are innocuous remedies which never do harm. . . . Even if it does no other good on some occasions than gain time, which often is the sole outcome, its employment would be commendable and useful to states, since it frequently takes only an instant to divert a storm.[10]

Richelieu, whom a contemporary wag described as negotiating the end of a war before hostilities had begun, believed that diplomatic negotiations and dialogue were so beneficial that they should not be interrupted even during war. This belief, shared by Butterfield, became part of the traditions of classical European statecraft before losing much of its relevance in the course of the twentieth century's world wars. Perhaps the most dramatic, and from Butterfield's viewpoint a most disastrous, modern instance of cutting off diplomacy in the midst of military conflict took place in World War II, when the Allies followed a policy of unconditional surrender towards Germany. Besides stiffening German resistance and discouraging domestic opposition to Hitler, the demand for unconditional surrender contributed mightily, as Butterfield regretfully noted, to the expansion of Russia into Eastern Europe, altering irreversibly perhaps the region's balance of power in her favor. Richelieu's and Butterfield's counsel implies that even in a relationship as charged with hostility and suspiciousness as that between the United States and the Soviet Union, active diplomacy in the form of ceaseless dialogue and continuous negotiation is an integral component of prudent statecraft that could serve the interests of both countries effectively.

A third means for the statesman to moderate the stark predicament at the heart of international conflict was the notion of an international order, closely related to the operation of the balance of power and diplomacy. As statesmen resorted to the balance of power and diplomacy, they often became aware of common interests transcending the rivalries among their states. Eventually, they began to think in terms of an international order to which they all belonged and the preservation of which contributed to the security and prosperity of its members. A "reason of system" evolved, complementing and providing inducements for the accommodation of the numerous "reasons of states." An international order resembled a club in that, while its members' rivalries continued, there was general agreement on some of the rules by which the competition should be carried out. The Great Powers of nineteenth-century Europe, to use Butterfield's analogy, may have competed "for the best armchairs or the best service at dinner," but they were determined "that the club itself should not be destroyed; all the parties being aware that such a catastrophe would only take away the value of the very things they were fighting about."[11] Like a club, an international order developed its own rules and institutions for the management of conflict. Some of the rules, embodied in international law, were explicit, while others, such as the code of behavior of diplomats and the series of maxims underlying European diplomacy until 1914, were in the form of an unwritten gentlemen's agreement but were no less authoritative.

The balance of power contributed to the growth of an international order in several ways. The balance prevented a single state from controlling the rest, laying the foundations for the idea of a family or concert of powers. It also encouraged statesmen to think in terms of long-term rather than short-term objectives, so that a state's self-interest could become more enlightened and less narrowly construed. After their initial exploits were limited by the operation of the balance of power, Frederick the Great and Bismarck became conservative statesmen solicitous for the preservation of the international order. They realized that further attempts at territorial expansion on their part would bring about a regrouping of the European powers against them. The conquest of Silesia or Germany's unification under Prussian leadership would be most secure over the long run if Prussia accepted the responsibilities of her membership in the European order and did not embark on a course of unlimited mastery. Thus, at least for Bismarck, though unfortunately not for his successors, Prussia's and Germany's national interest became linked with the preservation of a stable European equilibrium in which Germany was not so expansive or aggressive as to cause all other members of the system to fear and oppose her.

Diplomacy made an equally important contribution to the growth of an international order. As "power gives way to diplomacy, diplomacy in turn becomes more urbane, the diplomatic profession develops into an international society, and morality itself comes to have its place amongst the recognized conditions of intercourse between states."[12] Unlike Francisco de Vitoria and his distinguished successors, who sought to tame international politics through the direct application of religious, ethical, and legal norms, Butterfield believed that such norms and the international order they represented could grow in authoritativeness only gradually and after the struggle for power among states had been brought under control through the institutions of the balance of power and diplomacy. By promoting the dialogue among states, diplomacy revealed opportunities for accommodation and the existence of common interests, reminding statesmen of their nations' membership in a common international order or society.

As the international order of eighteenth- and nineteenth-century Europe developed, practitioners and theorists of diplomacy elaborated a series of maxims designed to preserve that delicately wrought community of interests within which the European states found long-term protection for their independence and general welfare. Interspersed throughout the writings of Callières, Frederick the Great, Burke, Gentz, Heeren, Talleyrand, Metternich, and Bismarck, these were the same maxims which Butterfield associated with an awareness of Providence and of the limits to human power. The maxims defined a moderate statecraft, through which statesmen could protect their states' vital interests without causing unlimited damage to the international order.[13]

Butterfield was aware of the political ambiguities connected with the idea of an international order. He knew that "the mechanical construction of a League of Nations or U.N.O. does not itself amount to an international order," and that one of the mistakes of twentieth-century Western liberalism was "the assumption that there exists an international order—with such claims on the individual members as an achieved international order might have—when such a thing is by no means an established fact."[14] A statesman whose diplomacy relied heavily on the existence of common interests and a minimal common morality among various states was likely to endanger his country's safety if, by a misperception of reality, he assumed the presence of an international order where there was none. Thus, the striving after an international order could be the source of grave disorders in world politics.

On the other hand, Butterfield thought that, even in the difficult political climate of the late twentieth century, a prudent but persistent effort to build an international order on the part of the United States, Western Europe, and Japan could have a gradual civilizing influence on the rhetoric, methods, and goals of the foreign policies of other states in the international system, eventually transforming this system into something akin to an international order or society. "If there is not an international order, it ought to be our object to make one, up to whatever degree the materials allow," he wrote.[15] Whenever conducted with due regard for the security of one's state and the distribution of forces in the international system, the quest for an international order became not an option for the statesman but a responsibility. And it was on the states with the greater power and the greater concern for the evolution of a humane civilization that this responsibility fell heaviest; they had the wider opportunities for building an international order and they stood to reap the greatest benefits in the form of increased international stability and a more secure environment for the development of humane values.

As effective as the balance of power, diplomacy, and the notion of an international order were in channelling the course of international politics along a more civilized course, Butterfield knew they were not foolproof. The always uneasy tension between reason of state and reason of system, between the pressing demands of the national interests and the requirements for an international order, sometimes unravelled into an anarchic scramble for short-term individual gains at the expense of the system's well-being, much as in Rousseau's classic parable of the stag hunt or as it happened during the course of World War I. Was there any way, then, short of a world empire, of permanently transcending the Hobbesian quagmire? Butterfield's answer was an unequivocal no. "For moral reasons human beings are incapable of permanently establishing a system of human relations on this earth such as can go on indefinitely without resort to violence."[16] Human cupidity was so pervasive that even the finest designs for international harmony eventually disintegrated into chaos and the struggle of all against all under the awesome pressures of egoism. For those not content with anything short of the eventual realization of a secular utopia, Butterfield's answer was disappointing.

But for the rest of mankind, including the prudent statesman, Butterfield offered some hope. By combining the creative exercise of his imagination with the taking of a calculated risk at that critical moment when the deadlock among nations assumed its apparent intractability, a statesman could help his nation to break out of the ring of fear into which international politics tends to degenerate.[17] This was no easy task, but, if the statesman succeeded in rising to the challenge of the historical moment, his bold and imaginative statecraft could bring the fruits of peace and a civilized existence to one or more generations. Considering the tragic world in which we live, this would be no small achievement.

Whether it was Bismarck negotiating the Reinsurance Treaty with Russia, Henry Kissinger and Richard Nixon searching for detente with the Soviet Union, or Anwar Sadat journeying to Jerusalem to end the bitter Egyptian-Israeli enmity, there was a similarity to their patterns of statecraft which Butterfield could not fail to notice and admire. These statesmen, none of whom could be called utopian liberals oblivious to the realities of power, had turned their position of strength into an opportunity for offering to their rivals accommodation and a relaxation of tensions. Their calculated risks, though insufficient to put their respective nations in deadly jeopardy, had been costly;

by comparison with the advantages to be gained, however, the short-term costs of the risk were worth bearing to this kind of bold, imaginative statesman. By taking such a costly but nonetheless limited risk, by discovering and putting to creative use the margin of security great powers often have, the Butterfieldian statesman could make the difference between a functioning international order and a general breakdown in which there were only losers.

7

Order and politics in the
twentieth century

The turbulent course of international affairs in his lifetime provided Butterfield with an unmatched opportunity to develop and apply to contemporary events his broad understanding of politics and wise statecraft. What Butterfield wrote in *The Origins of History* concerning Thucydides was true of himself as well: it is during catastrophic and tumultuous periods of history that historians are most frequently moved to profound reflection on the nature of international relations.[1]

Although he was only a boy when World War I broke out, the great cataclysm and the far-reaching changes it brought about in British society and Europe's political climate left an indelible mark on the young Butterfield. Decades later, as a mature historian, he often pondered in Burkean fashion whether such a radical and disastrous break in the continuity of European civilization had been inevitable or whether, through the creative statesmanship and vision of a few individuals, it could have been averted. Among the numerous aspects of this question that occupied his attention, he focused on the role played by the British foreign secretary, Sir Edward Grey, during the fateful decade preceding the war. Since the period of European diplomacy in which Grey was so intimately involved led to the destruction of the long-standing European order, Butterfield's probings also revealed ways in which the existence of the international order, its balance of power, and diplomacy might have been fruitfully prolonged if the statesmen of that time—or perhaps even one of them—had displayed a slightly greater degree of political creativity. Apart from its value to historians, Butterfield's study of Sir Edward Grey, which he did not complete until the mid-1960s, yielded insights into Butterfield's conception of wise statecraft that are useful to the student of diplomacy.[2]

According to Butterfield, the decisive shift in British policy toward Germany took place barely less than a decade before World War I. Russia's defeat by Japan in 1904–5 and her subsequent revolution left her temporarily absent from the map of European forces; German power appeared correspondingly more menacing than before. In 1907 Sir Eyre Crowe produced his famous memorandum for the British Foreign Office, claiming that Germany was making a bid for European hegemony which had to be resisted by Great Britain in concert with France and Russia. Around the same time, men with an anti-German orientation, including Charles Hardinge, Francis Bertie, and Arthur Nicolson, gained positions of prominence at the Foreign Office. When the former permanent under-secretary, Lord Sanderson, wrote a counter-memorandum in response to Crowe's, offering what Butterfield called "a more historical explanation of German policy" and pointing to "Britain's unimaginativeness as partly responsible for some of the difficulties that had arisen," his views were promptly dismissed.[3]

The debate within the Foreign Office between Crowe's and Sanderson's assessments of German foreign policy was, in fact, the subject of a separate study by Butterfield, deserving of a brief digression here.[4] In that paper, Butterfield contrasted what he considered the more historical approach of Sanderson towards the German problem with Crowe's interpretation. He used the two memoranda as examples of the profound differences in political analysis and prescription which can result from different readings of the historical process. Both Crowe and Sanderson used history heavily in trying to persuade their readers. And, as Butterfield put it, in both memoranda "the discussion of history slides so easily into the consideration of policy as to suggest that one's attitude to the past is hardly to be separated from the question of what one is wanting to do with the world." But, whereas Sanderson seemed to see the historical process as rather open-ended and flexible, so that in his view Germany's behavior was no different than that of similar Great Powers and therefore there were meaningful prospects of negotiation and accommodation with her, Crowe saw the German challenge as less susceptible to redirection and requiring an immediate halt. Crowe focused on the German naval buildup, her colonial expansion, her uncooperative diplomatic behavior towards Great Britain, and her military preponderance with respect to France. He saw in these the markings of a power ready to embark on the quest for world dominion. Sanderson pointed instead to Germany's recent entrance into the circle of the Great Powers after a long struggle to gain her national identity as an explanation for her diplomatic brashness and sense of insecurity. He reminded his readers that, in the race for colonies since 1871, the Germans had fared less well than the French or the British. He argued that until recently the French, rather than the Germans, had presented the greatest threat to British interests and that over the long pull Russia, not Germany, would pose the most demanding challenge to British diplomacy. And he charged the British with being too obtuse and pharisaical in not perceiving that Germany had genuine reasons for concern over her security in view of Russia's growing population and industrial-military resources. Butterfield thought that, of the two analyses, Sanderson's was a sounder foundation for policy because of its catholicity and long-term perspective. In underlining the possibility of resolving Anglo-German differences through negotiation, Sanderson's memorandum rested on "a more dynamic view of the time-process" and on the assumption that "all Great Powers are naturally striving to expand."

The Sanderson-Crowe debate, of course, is reminiscent of contemporary debates about the nature of Soviet foreign policy and the kind of response it should elicit from the Western alliance. Regardless of the position one takes on that debate, or on the older debate between Sanderson and Crowe, it is important to point out, as Butterfield did, the role played in such debates by different historical evaluations of what are essentially the same contemporary or recent political developments. The sharply divergent assessments of current Soviet policy offered by Richard Pipes and Stephen Cohen, for example, immediately come to mind, as do also the different readings by Alexander Solzhenitsyn and George F. Kennan of Russian history and of the world's future.

Butterfield's preference for Sanderson's supposedly broader and more careful reading of history as a foundation for policy did not imply that in Butterfield's view a diplomat had to be only a good, objective historian in order to do his work properly. While historical breadth and a flexible view of historical evolution were essential prerequisites, a diplomat had to go beyond these because ultimately he had to make concrete political decisions favorable to his country's interests. As he explained,

> If certain safeguards are overlooked, a statesman can fall into error through too great a capacity for understanding the other party, or too great a desire to understand. If this is his one aspiration, he had much better give himself to the trade of an historian. It can hardly be true in the absolute that the statesman can have too comprehensive an understanding; but the capacity to see the other party's point of view sympathetically may be disastrous to him unless his mind embraces wider considerations still.[5]

To return to Sir Edward Grey, his suspiciousness towards Germany coincided with a British desire for better relations with Russia for, despite the Far Eastern debacle of 1905, Russia continued to threaten the British Empire in Persia, Afghanistan, and India. Several key members of the Foreign Office, including Grey himself, believed that this threat would only grow with time, as Russia recovered her political will and military capabilities. Hence, when in 1907 Great Britain and Russia reached an agreement delimiting each other's spheres of influence in Persia, British policymakers eagerly expected Russia to deflect her ambitions away from the British Empire to other parts of the globe, such as the Balkans, where Britain supposedly had few vital interests. Obviously disagreeing with the focus of A. J. P. Taylor and other historians on German aggressiveness, Butterfield wrote that, by 1914, if one had to look for "a really aggressive movement in Europe . . . one would have to point to the Serbo-Russian activity in the Balkans which was known to involve the actual breakup of the Austro-Hungarian Empire."[6]

In addition to threatening Austria's integrity, Russia's forward policy in the Balkans contained the risk of a general European war, since neither France nor Germany would allow the power and prestige of their respective allies, Russia and Austria, to suffer a major setback. In response to the growing tension between the Austro-German and Franco-Russian blocs, Britain could have played her time-honored role of preserving the European balance of power by acting as mediator between the two opposing alliances. Yet British policy towards Russia made this impossible because Great Britain, afraid of Russia's growing power, was eager to support Russia in the Balkans and Turkey, in exchange for some breathing space in India and Persia.

Butterfield was sharply critical of Grey's Russian policy. Its implications for Austria were devastating and, since Austria was a fundamental pillar of the European balance of power and the international order from which Britain derived immense benefits, the consequences were likely to be adverse to British interests also. The historian Paul W. Schroeder, a recognized authority on Central European history, has developed this theme very persuasively, noting that the blank check to Russia implicit in the British rapprochement amounted to a great failure of British diplomacy, and a flagrant disregard for the balance of power in Europe:

> Only the presence of the Habsburg Monarchy holding down the Danube basin kept Germany or Russia from achieving mastery over Europe. With Austria there and determined to remain an independent great power, it was very difficult for either of them to fight each other, or dominate the other, or combine for aggressive purposes. Let Austria go under, and a great war for the mastery of Europe became almost mathematically predictable. . . . Only a commitment by Britain to use her influence with France to help keep Austria in existence by maintaining a balance of power in the Balkans and restraining Austria, Russia and the Balkan states alike could have prevented this.[7]

Butterfield aimed at Grey and his colleagues with respect to Germany the same accusation levelled at them by Schroeder concerning Austria. They were insensitive to the delicate equilibrium maintained in Eastern Europe by the fairly even distribution of power between Germany and Russia. Troubled as they were by the pressing German threat of the moment, they were too unimaginative to see that, over the long run, Russia posed an even more disturbing challenge to the European order. "Once Russia achieved the ascendancy, she would have the better chance of rendering it permanent, the better chance of securing that a broken rival should never be able to reconstitute its power."[8] In the middle of the nineteenth century, Alexis de Tocqueville and the Austrian writer Julius Frobel had foreseen this eventuality. Neither before nor during the war did the British diplomatic establishment ask itself the question raised by Lord Morley in 1914, and which Butterfield considered critically important, "when you have dealt with Germany what are you going to do with Russia?" Only "the hand of Providence" in the form of the unexpected Revolution and Civil War of 1917–21 kept Russia from emerging out of World War I as the dominant continental power in control of Eastern Europe and the Straits.[9]

A flexible and creative British diplomacy would have addressed itself to the dual problem of restraining German ambitions and forestalling the ongoing expansion of Russian power. Such a diplomacy would have exerted vigorous efforts in keeping the peace between the adversary blocs, because a war between Germany and Russia was likely to upset the delicate balance in Eastern Europe regardless of who was the victor. To act as arbiter, Great Britain would have needed a better understanding of the serious strategic anxieties at the heart of German foreign policy. Unfortunately, the Crowe memorandum of 1907 was still an important theoretical foundation of the Foreign Office's diplomacy six years later, despite the massive growth of Russian power and French assertiveness that had taken place in those years. As Butterfield argued, "British diplomats (and later historians) were unwilling or unable to see that Germany might have a genuine fear of Russia, and that this might account for some elements of intransigence in her policy that seemed unreasonable."[10] Had the British understood better this fear, they might have been able to anticipate the preventive war launched by Austria and Germany in 1914, and their diplomacy might have been fashioned to avert such a development.

But Sir Edward Grey, wrote Butterfield, did not work "from any comprehensive map of European forces, or with any historical sense for the relationship between Germany and Russia."[11] This was a case in which a statesman could have profited from a deeper understanding of the international system's political history and of the traditional roles played by the various powers, including his country's antagonists, in maintaining the system's general equilibrium. Grey and his colleagues were mainly concerned with and unduly blinded by the German threat to France and, insofar as they had a Russian policy, it was one bordering on appeasement. Their failure of imagination was so great that they consistently underestimated the strength of Great Britain's diplomatic position and her capacity to act as arbiter if she chose to do so. Right up to the outbreak of war, France and Russia repeatedly hinted that unless England supported the entente more decisively they would desert her. Butterfield was amazed by the weight which this veiled threat carried in the minds of Grey, Nicolson, and other top officials; in reality, between 1912 and 1914 Great Britain's need of the continental states' support was far less than the need of both opposing groups for what she could offer to them. Excessive fear and anxiety, combined with a failure of catholicity of thought, blurred these officials' vision and obscured the rich possibilities open to British diplomacy.

Grey—and this was one of the areas in which perhaps the study of history might have been helpful to him—did not see the configuration of political forces in Europe as fluid or subject to evolution. Had he done so, his diplomacy might have been more flexible. It would not have had as its overriding goal the immediate control of German expansion. The latter would have been only one among other objectives, which would have included also the preservation of Austria and the management of the general European equilibrium to prevent Russia from ever gaining the ascendancy to which her size seemed naturally to impel her. Grey also lacked the imagination and boldness to take a calculated risk, which alone could have broken the increasingly vicious deadlock between the adversary alliances. "England, if she had been only a little less clearly committed, might have provided for some years the one loop-hole for the admission of greater flexibility into the diplomatic situation."[12] Butterfield credits Grey with a genuine desire to act as mediator when the final crisis came, but by then it was probably too late. "His persuasions might have been different but his actual *will* might have had greater weight with both the Triple Alliance and the Entente powers in 1914, but for certain aspects of his earlier policy for which he rather than the cabinet had been responsible."[13]

During the critical last week of July 1914, the British fear of what might happen to Great Britain if, as a result of lukewarm support for Russia, the latter deserted her, affected the course of Grey's diplomacy making it extremely difficult for him to restrain St. Petersburg. Early in that week, for example, the reasoning cropped up in an important minute to the Foreign Office from the British ambassador to Russia, Sir George Buchanan, that if Great Britain did not stand by Russia in this crisis, and if Russia and France defeated Germany in war without British assistance, the British Empire should anticipate future troubles in India. The implication here, as in the earlier arguments of Grey and Nicolson for a pro-Russian course, was that Russia would not channel her future aggressiveness towards Great Britain if the latter assisted Russia immediately. The British policymakers were indulging in the illusion, with which Butterfield charged Machiavelli, of supposing that the difficult task of preserving a balance of power between two factions could be evaded by supporting one faction and then counting on its gratitude after one's aid had helped it to achieve preeminence. Without disguising his acerbity, Butterfield commented, "Diplomacy is no longer diplomacy if, when aggression is in question, the issue pivots finally on such an act of faith or such a piece of sentimentality." [14]

In his history of World War I, Sir Winston Churchill, as sensitive as Butterfield to the tragic element in international conflict and to the tension between necessity and freedom that underlies the statesman's work, asked pointedly: "Could we in England perhaps by some effort, by some sacrifice of our material interests, by some compulsive gesture, at once in friendship and command, have reconciled France and Germany in time and formed that grand association on which alone the peace and glory of Europe would be safe?" [15] Regardless of their relatively peripheral difference of opinion on the issue of whether the Franco-German or the Russo-German clash was the key problem of British diplomacy, both Churchill and Butterfield were concerned with the profound question of whether a statesman can transcend, even if only temporarily, the dreadful Hobbesian dilemma in which he functions by replacing the pressing short-term interests crowded around him with a broader vision of the future. Like Butterfield, Churchill recognized that such a statesman would need to blend a creative imagination, including the risk of temporary material advantages that always seem so painful to yield, with a bold act of free will "at once of friendship and command."

Butterfield's conception of wise statecraft directs the statesman to avoid the equally dangerous temptations of utopianism and nihilism. The statesman must face the problem of power unflinchingly. In his work the sentimentalities of British policy towards Russia prior to 1914 have no place; nor is there room for the more common illusions of utopian liberals who hope to escape from the rigorous demands of the balance of power. Only by immersing himself in power politics can the statesman soften their grip on man. Thus, the task of statecraft ought to be the feasible one of managing power politics rather than the illusory one of trying to abolish them.

The wise statesman also realizes, however, that the wisdom of politics does not achieve its fulfillment in the lust for power animating a state's foreign policy. Unless broadened to include the interests of the international order within which the state exists, as well as the interests of future generations, a state's self-interest becomes sterile and destructive of its higher purposes. Therefore, while political wisdom encompasses power politics, it does so in order to direct them towards more meaningful and humane aims than the mere accumulation of power for its own sake. Such aims include a tolerably civilized international order, as well as the attainment of some degree of order, peace, and felicity for the millions of human beings constituting the state's reason for being. Butterfield's conception of wise statecraft is thus permeated with a moral purpose, and the severe realism underlying this state-craft only increases the authenticity and force of its moral vision.

Despite the opportunities open to them, the statesmen of 1914 failed to guide their power politics by that broader imaginative vision of the common good that could have made the difference between the chaos that ensued, of which we are the reluctant heirs, and an international order more capable of sustaining a humane civilization. As Schroeder lamented, in words with which Butterfield would have agreed:

> The attitudes behind it all, in any case, were universal—the same short-sighted selfishness and lack of imagination, the same ex-clusive concentration on one's own interests at the expense of the community. Everyone wanted a payoff; no one wanted to pay. Everyone expected the system to work for him; no one would work for it. . . . All believed, as many historians still do, that *sacro egoismo* is the only rational rule for high politics, that it really represents a higher realism and a higher morality, when it really is only a higher stupidity. And so the system was bent and twisted until it broke; its burdens were distributed not according to ability to bear them, but inability to resist. Inevitably the collapse came where all the weight was concentrated—at the weakest point.[16]

Like Sir Eyre Crowe and others in the British Foreign Office, Grey was guilty of historical narrowness and of unimaginativeness with respect to Germany's fear and Great Britain's opportunity to break the deadlock between the opposing camps. His sins of omission, like those of the other European statesmen at the time, cost Europe dearly, their consequences haunting us to this day.

Although he followed the events of the twenties, the thir-ties, and World War II with great interest, Butterfield wrote very little about them. Even in its halcyon days, the League of Nations with all the utopian misconceptions it helped to engender failed to rouse any enthusiasm on But-terfield's part. Although he had no sympathy for Nazism, he saw its policies of national self-assertion as the result of a predictable reaction by a great number of Germans against the Versailles settlement and the glib, sterile lib-eralism still prevailing in much of the West. Even after World War II broke out, Butterfield did not allow his dislike of Hitler to obscure his political vision. He constantly maintained the distinction between the Nazi govern-ment and the German nation, surmising that when the war was over Western Europe would need a strong, prosperous Germany as a bulwark against Rus-sia and a pillar of whatever international order came into being. For this reason, the policy of unconditional surrender followed by Churchill exasperated him, as did the intense anti-German rhetoric and propaganda of the war years. For the second time in the twentieth century, a war which it was in the best interests of Great Britain to limit had been allowed to turn into an unlimited "War for Righteousness," with British statesmen bearing a share of responsibility for the transformation. Out of the ensuing disorder and the weakening of British and German power, Russia had emerged as the chief beneficiary.

After 1945, feeling perhaps that by then he was sufficiently well established in his profession, Butterfield began to write more about contemporary affairs. The tragic denouement of World War II, the opportunities presented to Christianity by a world more aware of its own brokenness, and the stirrings of bitter enmity among the victorious powers that not long before had been fraternal allies supplied him with powerful themes for reflection. He was now a mature scholar and thinker, bringing to his probings of international politics a sharp Christian realism and the political and historical understanding born of several major studies of Napoleon and Machiavelli. His observations of the cold war, a struggle which to this day is the salient motif of international politics whether in the harsh tone of the arms race or the more modulated ones of detente, remain a valuable point of reference for students and practitioners of international relations alike.

For Butterfield, the origins of the cold war owed less to the Soviet Union's communist ideology than to the enormous power and territory it had gained during World War II. Writing in early 1949, he observed: "If, on the present territorial distribution, Russia had still been Tsarist Russia, even the inefficient Tsarist Russia, and even a Christian state amongst other Christian states in the traditional sense, I should regard the danger as greater than anything in modern history . . . since the Mongols."[17] It was a grave mistake for the free world to define the Russian menace in primarily ideological terms. The open societies of the West, with their share of social and economic flaws, devoted to a somewhat ambiguous vision of the good society, seemed a poor match for a Marxist ideology that promised the full satisfaction of man's deepest longings through the establishment of justice and equality for all. Instead, Western diplomacy should draw attention to Russia's lust for power and aggrandizement, which threatened the independence of even those nations with socialist regimes.

Butterfield put forth these arguments in a 1949 letter to his friend, the British diplomat Adam Watson, who, shortly after he received it, circulated it in the British Foreign Office, where it was read with sympathetic interest. The letter foreshadowed the policy adopted by the Western alliance when it extended military aid to Yugoslavia in 1950, following Tito's break with Moscow in 1948. Butterfield's logic also dictated a course such as Great Britain followed towards Communist China after the collapse of the nationalist regime, but which the United States did not adopt until 1972. Influenced as he was by the reasoning of classical statecraft, Butterfield considered it problematical to enmesh one's foreign policy in ideological spider webs and much more effective to conduct such policy in accordance with time-tested ideas of common interests and concern for the balance of power. This way of thinking may be shared to some extent by contemporary leaders of Communist China who in recent years have appealed to the Western alliance for support in making a common front against Soviet hegemonism.

As the decade of the fifties unrolled and the old colonial empires crumbled, the spectacle of a large group of new nations uncommitted to either the Western or the Soviet blocs gave Butterfield's arguments for a non-ideological diplomacy fresh cogency. The new nations, representing a significant portion of mankind and endowed with large stores of the world's resources, would make their influence felt in world affairs sooner or later. Hence, it was of critical importance to prevent them from throwing their weight on the side of the Soviet bloc. In this task a Western ideological diplomacy was at a disadvantage for two reasons. First, pronouncements on behalf of democracy and freedom would be of dubious credibility, proceeding from powers that only a few years before had kept these nations in colonial submission and who still maintained a much resented economic and cultural dominance. Second, Marxism had great appeal for the newly liberated peoples, many of whom were likely to flirt with it, some of them adapting it to local circumstances and others discarding it after finding out for themselves that it did not suit their needs.

A Western diplomacy that emphasized the ideological differences between the Soviet and Western blocs ran the risk of creating in the minds of the Third World peoples a positive association between their economic aspirations, which lent themselves easily to a Marxist frame of reference anyway, and the power of the Soviet Union to help fulfill those aspirations. To put it mildly, such diplomacy would be disastrous. It would be much better, argued Butterfield, to leave the issue of ideology, on which the West's position was weakest, aside and to disentangle Marxism, with its rich emotional appeal, from the image of the Soviet Union drawn by Western propaganda. The Soviets should be presented as mere power grabbers, as skillful imitators of and successors to the old colonialist powers, who threatened the independence and national pride of the new nations.[18]

If there was a moral vision that the foreign policy of the West had to offer, it should be that of a pluralistic world in which socialist, capitalist, and other states could exist as members of the same international order. Butterfield was confident that, in the end, this derivation of the principle of self-determination would carry greater weight with the Third World peoples than any sentimental attachments to the Soviet Union based on the latter's sup-

posed faithfulness to Marxist ideals. The new nations would be more attracted to the vision of a world where each of them could follow whichever
way of life it chose, including even socialism, than to the homogeneous
world order espoused by the Soviets, where ideological harmony would only
strengthen the Soviets' capacity to interfere with the independence of weaker
states.

In Butterfield's mind, the mistakes of Allied diplomacy during the
Napoleonic Wars provided an excellent illustration of the problem he was
addressing. Throughout the French Revolution and the first years of Napoleon's rule, the European powers opposed to France's expansion had stressed
the need to contain the revolution and preserve the European political and
social order as it existed. This had the effect of drawing towards France
peoples, such as the Italians and Germans, who wanted to see the old order
pass away. Only later did the Allies begin to play their strongest card, the
fear on the part of all European peoples that Napoleon, under the banner of
the revolution's ideology, intended to become master of the continent.

With respect to the Third World at least, Butterfield's case for a non-
ideological diplomacy has been strengthened by events of the past two decades. The new nations appear to prize their self-determination and national
sovereignty more than any links with the Soviet Union resulting from socialist solidarity. Whenever Soviet power has seemed to become a threat to
their independence, most Third World nations have not hesitated to cut the
Soviet tie and turn to the West for help in pursuing socialist as well as non-
socialist development strategies.

In 1954 the explosion of the first hydrogen bomb—at that time, the
most destructive weapon ever devised by man—as well as the continuing
tension in East-West relations, sparked within Butterfield a series of further reflections on international politics. During these years the cold war
seemed at its height: John Foster Dulles was United States secretary of state,
Khrushchev threatened the West at least once with "a rain of nuclear bombs
on London and Paris," and the Berlin crisis brewed feverishly. Even in this
inauspicious political climate, Butterfield foresaw, as indeed he had done
since at least 1949, the possibility of a detente between the two antagonist
blocs.

A detente, as in previous centuries, might come about through sheer
exhaustion, because neither side was willing to surrender its principles yet
neither had the strength to overcome the other. Sooner or later men would
grow weary of the high tension in which they constantly lived and would seek
a temporary relaxation, a truce. As its benefits became more widely perceived, the truce, which at first would have been seen as a shameful but necessary respite, would become permanent and valued as a good in itself. Each
side would remain committed to its ideology and vision of the world's future,

especially in its rhetoric and official pronouncements, but in practice they would recognize each other's right to exist in the same world. Conflict would not disappear, but the frighteningly high level of tension and the rigid alignments within each camp might give way to more flexible relationships, varied plays of interests, opportunities for compromise, and a mellowing of the harsh ideological warfare that was so denigrating to the human soul. As time passed, a new international order might arise in which nations, despite their different regimes and conflicts of interests, recognized the legitimacy of each other's membership in the same "club." Such had been the evolution of Europe from the religious wars of the sixteenth century down to the highly sophisticated international order of the eighteenth, and it was this historical analogy above all that inspired Butterfield's reflections throughout the 1950s and 1960s on the future possibilities open to the West's foreign policy.[19] He reassured those who argued that only an all-out war against the Soviet Union would solve the West's political dilemma, that "the human predicament in the twentieth century would not be greatly or enduringly altered if Russia and even communism were to disappear entirely from the map. The forces would certainly reshuffle themselves, and the pattern would change, but the fundamental problem would not be solved."[20] But then, as if for the liberals' benefit, he also warned that "even a detente, though desirable and not impossible, would not eliminate the predicament; and if one party were to be misled by it—hoaxed into taking off the safeguards and abandoning its vigilance while the other were unremittingly alert—the result could be an irreversible misfortune."[21]

Meanwhile, the ongoing development of highly destructive nuclear weapons in the fifties moved him in what perhaps was the most controversial direction his thought ever took. The growing stockpiles of nuclear weapons on either side of the iron curtain were evidence of the tragic predicament in which East and West were locked. The governments of the Western Alliance, immersed in "the dominion of fear," seemed wholly controlled by the rule of necessity. In such circumstances the policies of a balance of power—a strategic nuclear balance coupled with a conventional one—cautious diplomacy, and the search for a new international order through the slow unfolding of detente, seemed—and to many sensible observers still seem—the only alternatives worth pursuing. But surprisingly, for Butterfield, the tough-minded theorist of classical statecraft, these policies were insufficient to untie the Gordian knot of the nuclear arms race. A bolder policy was required.

Butterfield always had recognized that, despite their overall effectiveness, the limited mechanisms of the balance of power, diplomacy, and the structures of an international order sometimes failed to keep the peace and actually intensified the Hobbesian fear gripping nations, leading them to catastrophic war. His study of the origins of World War I had made him even more conscious than before of this sad reality, further persuading him that these traditional instruments of statecraft had to be complemented by the bold and imaginative statesman who, when the deadlock of wills seemed most intractable, broke the grip of necessity and conditioning circumstances on policy through a mighty act of volition. In the age of nuclear weapons, such an act was imperative because, whereas the world could recover from the religious wars of the past or even two world wars, human life itself might be imperilled by a general nuclear conflict. A "strong human affirmation . . . may be the only way of . . . deflecting the course of development to which we are now enslaved." He had in mind nothing less than a decision by the West not to manufacture, store, or ever use strategic nuclear weapons.[22]

Before rushing to prove Butterfield wrong on this issue, one should give him a hearing. As a student of human nature and a historian, he feared what most of us refuse even to contemplate: that, sooner or later and despite elaborate efforts to avoid it, nuclear weapons would be used in war, devastating our planet. This horrifying prospect put upon every government the obligation of doing whatever was within its reach to rid the world of the atomic curse. In response to critics like Raymond Aron, who pointed out that unilateral nuclear renunciation would bring about centuries of subjugation under Soviet totalitarian despotism, Butterfield argued that "with modern nuclear weapons we could easily put civilization back a thousand years, while the course of a single century can produce a colossal transition from despotic regimes to a system of liberty." This was the voice of a historian deeply conscious of the vast changes and unexpected turns which the human spirit can bring about in history. To those like the theologian Reinhold Niebuhr, who agreed that nations had the right to use atomic weapons in self-defense, Butterfield put the question of "whether there is no conceivable weapon that we will brand as an atrocity, whether there is no horror that we should regard as impermissible for the winning of a war, because so uncommensurate with the limited objects that can ever be secured by war." This was the query of a Christian challenging the implacable grip of necessity on foreign policy from the perspective of divine eternity. "When there is a terrible *impasse*, it is sometimes useless to go on battering against the obstruction—one must play a trick on fatality by introducing a new factor into the case. . . . Let us take the devil by the rear, and surprise him with a dose of those gentler virtues that will be poison to him. At least when the world is in extremities, the doctrine of love becomes the ultimate measure of our conduct."[23]

Butterfield's associates in the British Committee on the Theory of International Politics, especially Adam Watson, gradually persuaded him to abandon his stance in favor of unilateral nuclear disarmament. By 1968, he no longer called for unilateral renunciation but simply for a policy statement by the West that it never would be the first to use atomic weapons. He continued to think that a détente was essential, although he knew that it would not do away with all conflict between East and West, and that it would require the Western Alliance to maintain a strong military posture. He described in detail the best way to bring about this détente and the kind of statesman needed for the task:

> One could conceive the next step in progress to be one which would involve a crucial act of faith in human nature, in spite of all that has been said about the limitations of this latter. It would be a thing not without risk—a risk which itself would have to be a measure that could be achieved only by a state that would be acting from a position of power. It is not the young men or the academic people or the wishful-thinkers who would ever be able to measure the chances of it; and those who merely consider the struggle as a straight war of right against wrong would never entertain the idea at all. For such an object it would almost be better to confide all that one values to the good intentions of a Bismarck, in spite of all his offences—confide it to a Bismarck at his best. There could be no higher act of statesmanship than this, and no act that could ever require a more creative statesmanship.[24]

He had in mind what the historian John Lewis Gaddis was to call later "tough détente." When, a few years after the above words were written, the United States initiated a rapprochement with the Soviet Union, Butterfield saw in Henry Kissinger's work a partial fulfillment of his expectations.[25]

Butterfield's counsel to the West to pursue a nonideological diplomacy modelled along the lines of classical, pre-World War I statecraft and his insistence that the West strive for the creation of a pluralistic international order are vulnerable to the kind of criticism directed by Raymond Aron in 1954 against George Kennan and Hans Morgenthau, that they were

> right in warning us against a tendency to let ourselves be carried away by blind ideological fury. But they make the radical error of mistaking for the essence of world politics a set of practices and a theory characteristic of those happy eras when within a stabilized civilization an unwritten code of legitimacy and illegitimacy sets limits to the contests of states—both to the means states use and to the consequences of their contests. When such a code is missing we are back in a state of nature where freedom and existence are at stake, where the clashing communities mobilize all their resources because they stake all their goods and their very life in the struggle. It takes two to negotiate a settlement; both sides must speak the same language and follow the same principles. To suggest that one

should behave toward an Empire animated by a secular religion in the same way as one behaved toward Czarist Russia, to ignore how different Nazi Germany was from Wilhelm's Germany is very much the opposite of realism and could lead to the disaster one seeks to avoid. It is legitimate that one should lament the passing of those centuries when diplomacy, divorced from ideas and morality, limited itself to a subtle game of influence and power. But in the twentieth century, a great power weakens itself if it refuses to serve an idea.[26]

Several arguments can be raised on Butterfield's behalf. First, he did not say that the foreign policy of the West should be nonideological in the sense of refusing to serve an idea; what he said was that the idea should be pluralism, rather than notions such as democracy, capitalism, or human rights, which were likely to cause more fragmentation than consensus in the world community. Moreover, the goal of pluralism was likely to put the Soviets and their allies on the defensive. Either they rejected pluralism, in which case they would frighten away from their camp many of the developing nations, or else they had to accept pluralism, a move which implied the denial of the universality of Marxism and the legitimacy of other forms of society.

Second, Butterfield thought that, despite the vast ideological gulf separating the West from the Soviet Union, prudent diplomacy between the two blocs was feasible. He agreed with Churchill who, as early as 1948, had stated that although "it is idle to reason or argue with the Communists," it is "possible to deal with them on a fair, realistic basis, and, in my experience, they will keep their bargains as long as it is in their interest to do so." While the Soviets did not share the West's political principles, they spoke and understood the language of interests and power.[27]

Third, while Butterfield was aware of the dangers of overestimating the prospects for the creation and maintenance of a genuine international order, he also realized that the opportunities were there and that the West could take advantage of them without necessarily endangering its security or sacrificing its power. His answer to those who claimed that an international order in the late twentieth century was impossible because of the absence of a common framework of moral values between East and West was revealing: "I am prepared to start from the fact that international law, . . . international morality, and the international order do not exist; but this makes our discussion all the more important. We are creating these things, or refusing to create them, by the way in which we think about them now."[28]

If the West should take the lead it was because of its vast economic, political, and military resources and because it stood to reap the greatest benefits from an international order. An anarchic world torn by ideological struggles and military conflicts between East and West and their respective proxies was exactly the kind of world in which the Soviet Union could play most effectively its best two cards: its Marxist revolutionary ideology and its ability to foment political and military disorders of various magnitudes throughout the international system. By working towards the creation of an international order, the West would be shifting, however gradually, the co-ordinates of international relations towards areas where it could play its com-parative advantages: its vision of a pluralistic international system, its ability to give the developing nations substantial assistance, and the relative internal stability of its societies.

However insightful many of Butterfield's observations on the cold war were, an exception must be made for his stance on nuclear weapons. At least as articulated in its most radical version, it was a sharp departure from that prudence which, as he himself realized, ought to be at the heart of foreign policy. It is a credit to Butterfield that, unlike other advocates of unilateral nuclear renunciation, he had the intellectual courage to acknowledge that the consequences of his policy could well be the subjugation of Western Europe to Soviet power. He considered this risk preferable to that of utter annihila-tion. But he failed to state that his extreme counsel could not guarantee the future absence of a planetary nuclear holocaust. Western renunciation of nu-clear weapons could not prevent India, China, or other Third World states from developing these weapons and eventually plunging the world into the same nightmare Butterfield sought to avoid.

Perhaps human existence is much more tragic and international rela-tions a sadder affair than even Butterfield intimated. In the nuclear age, the statesman of a superpower has no other choice but to hold in his hands the terrifying weapons of doomsday in the hope that no adversary will be tempted to use his. By resolving that he will not be the first to use them, the statesman is already reaching the very limits of any possible faith in human nature—a faith which Butterfield recognized was also involved in even as calculated and limited a political move as a détente. Whereas Butterfield's writings in the late forties and early fifties had sought to reconcile Christianity with the realities of power politics and to educate thinking Christians accordingly, his later call for unilateral nuclear disarmament represented an astonishing, al-beit temporary, reversion to the alluring political simplicities of dissenting Christianity, a rather un-Augustinian flight from the tragedy of politics and power.[29]

As the second half of the twentieth century moved on, Butterfield saw in Christianity a great hope for improving the increasingly ominous prospects of nuclear war at the level of international relations and reversing the grow-ing dehumanization that threatened Western civilization from within. In both instances Christianity was most likely to succeed, not so much by capturing the imagination of a few brilliant intellectuals and statesmen but by working its subtle influences through the lives of those millions of "ordinary" human beings which elite creeds and ideologies generally have dismissed as inconsequential, but which the Church has regarded as precious in God's sight. As a Methodist and a historian, Butterfield was sensitive to the radical changes Christianity was capable of bringing about by quietly and unostentatiously transforming the daily habits and perceptions of the Everyman.

Within society, Christianity's uncompromising affirmation of the priceless value and dignity of the person could be a powerful barrier to reductionist, dehumanizing ideologies. And by reminding the average citizen of his sins and those of his nation, of the perils of self-righteousness and of man's universal brotherhood in Christ, Christianity also could ease the enormous pressures that mass cupidity and self-righteous chauvinism exert on a state's foreign policy.

The deadlock between opposing camps in international affairs could be broken if one side had sufficient imagination to realize what many have denied, that the adversary's fear was as genuine, and his predicament as difficult, as one's own. Perhaps only Christian love was capable of nurturing that kind of creative imagination. The love of God who died on the cross for man might enable a person to understand and feel to the depth of his being the awfulness of the tragedy into which his fellow human beings were imprisoned. When multiplied by millions and spread throughout an entire society, this creative imagination could be a powerful incentive to the statesman to take a bold risk and, in a gesture "at once of friendship and command," hold out to the adversary the possibility of temporary accommodation if not lasting reconciliation.

IV

The Wisdom of Christianity

So we have to picture the principles of our religion, and particularly New Testament Love or Christian charity, existing as a kind of fermentation in society, operating like something in chemistry, perpetually moving as a spontaneous and original spiritual force. . . . we can never tell what a man may not do when he says to himself "How shall I worship God?," and we can never tell what he may not do just for love. Something of Christianity, thrusting itself upwards in a Gothic cathedral, may add greater novelty to the landscape than all the imitators of the ancient Greeks. Medieval religion, working upon the philosophy of Aristotle, may produce more original results than Renaissance scholarship seeking to recover Aristotle neat. A mystical urge which drives a man to discover mathematical harmonies in the universe may lead to an astronomy beyond the imagination of those who are merely continuing the traditional methods of their science. Our religion, as it mixes with the events of the world, generates new things—now a kind of art, now a form of science, now humanism, now liberty, now a theory of egalitarianism.

Above all, throughout our history it has been of the first importance that our Church has not merely launched or inspired great human enterprises, only too often to watch them break away and sail off on their own account; it has not merely leavened society generally with its principles of Christian charity, for example, so that the enemies of religion have owed more to it than they have ever been able to recognize; but, by being here, the Church stands as a perpetual centre from which the whole process can be for ever starting over again. Those who preach the Gospel, nurse the pieties, spread New Testament Love, and affirm the spiritual nature of man are guarding the very fountain, dealing with the problems of civilization at its very source, and keeping open the spring from which new things will still arise. Compared with this contribution it is unimportant if they themselves make mistaken judgments on mundane issues in history. The continually renascent power of our religion seems to consist in this unlimited opportunity to return to the original spring, the original simplicities of the faith.

Herbert Butterfield

8

Christianity's challenge
to the contemporary world

As a devout Christian, Butterfield was greatly concerned with the possibilities open to Christianity in the late twentieth century and the influence it might have on the general political and intellectual climate underlying the course of international relations. As a student of European civilization intimately acquainted with Christianity's past, he also realized that any speculations on the future impact of the faith required an understanding not only of its philosophy and theology, but of its interactions with political and social institutions throughout its history as well.

In his analysis of Christianity, Butterfield maintained a sharp distinction between Christianity as a spiritual religion addressed to the innermost conscience of individual human beings and Christianity as "the bond of the tribe," as a religion which for over a thousand years had provided cultural, social, and political cohesiveness to a civilization and which relied for its support on habit and the power of the state. These two kinds of Christianity had coexisted, sometimes in uneasy tension, during much of the faith's history, and their relationships to one another had been the source of many dynamic developments in Western civilization.

For Butterfield it was significant that Christianity as a spiritual religion "made its appearance, and its implications were first developed, in a highly civilized world which had achieved an advanced form of urban life and had brought the human intellect to a refinement and subtlety never exceeded since."[1] Moreover, in its first three centuries, Christianity spread "over the length and breadth of the civilized world" solely through its power of persuasion, sometimes in the face of bitter persecution by the Roman authorities. Butterfield drew several implications. The Gospel had a powerful spiritual and intellectual appeal to man, which transcended the relativities of the historical process. Christianity did not need to ally itself with the secular power, and was even likely to compromise its credibility and integrity when it did so. In the late twentieth century, now that it had been finally stripped of its Constantinian alliance with the secular power and had to depend entirely on the spiritual substance of its message, Christianity, confronting a highly sophisticated and skeptical civilization not unlike the one where it first set its roots, had before it possibilities as exciting as those of its early days. Christendom might be on the wane, but Christianity had an open future filled with unpredictable opportunities.[2]

Constantine's conversion and Christianity's establishment as the official religion of the Roman Empire in the fifth century A.D. had marked the beginning of a period in which Christianity was to be "now the support, now the agent, now the suffering colleague, and now the passive accomplice of secular authority."[3] This active partnership continued with vigor after Rome's collapse. Most of the new barbarian monarchies that dotted Western Europe were quick to embrace Christianity as a politically and culturally useful legacy of Rome, indispensable for securing the acceptance of the populations that had formerly belonged to the Empire. Even during these centuries, commonly known as the Dark Ages, the spiritual substance of Christianity retained its integrity; yet it was often overshadowed in the world of political events by the workings of Christianity as an arm of the state, as an instrument of intellectual, social, and religious totalitarianism. Butterfield explained:

> A general unanimity in the Christian faith—or indeed in anything else that may be the subject of speculation—is a solemn and awful thing, not to be counted as ordinarily achievable in adult states of society without resort to methods that are grim to contemplate. The wholesale conversions of peoples after the downfall of imperial Rome were typical of a state of society and civilization in which the group did naturally predominate in matters of religion; and the warfare of Christianity against paganism at this time was a warfare not against modern freedom of thought but against the darker tyranny of mere barbarian custom. This backward state of things—this dominance of a more primitive kind of herd-spirit—was to continue even under Christianity, and it conditioned the character of the world in the succeeding centuries. And under these circumstances Christianity in one respect became a religion in a different sense of the word from that which we find in the New Testament—fulfilling a function in society which other religions, even pagan ones, have fulfilled at other times and places, when civilization has been in its early stages. It became, so to speak, the bond of the tribe—the very basis of such sense of unity as existed on the continent—and it established itself even as the fundamental principle which was supposed to hold kingdoms and nations together.[4]

While the Church participated in this process, it did not bear full responsibility for it. An explanation had to be sought also in the chaotic political conditions of the time, when societies had to resort to every available means of cohesion, including religion, in order to survive. Had Christianity not been around, pagan religions would have taken its place as "the bond of the tribe." In fact, by gradually educating the barbarians and softening their manners over the course of several centuries, the Church paved the way for a return to a more civilized order in which man could find his way out of the primitive totalitarianism of the Dark Ages. With its teaching on the value of the person and its emphasis on love, Christianity in its spiritual dimensions combined with improving economic and political conditions to help produce after 1000 A.D. the dynamic civilization of the Middle Ages which despite its outward religious uniformity gave to human beings greater room for diversity and freedom than they had experienced for many centuries.

For Butterfield one of the profoundest questions of European history was why the western half of the continent proved to be so much more dynamic than the east, "so much more capable of generating new things, and so pregnant with unexpected developments."[5] He thought that part of the answer was found in the relative independence which the Church had achieved in the West in relation to the secular power. The collapse of the Roman Empire freed the Church from the threat of any major encroachments on its integrity by a strong political authority. By the time political institutions regained their capacity to attempt to dominate the Church, the latter's authority was sufficiently well-established to enable her to resist the secular power effectively. The ensuing conflict between Church and state in the Middle Ages was beneficial because it "prevented on either side the establishment of a cramping totalitarianism," contributing greatly to the spiritual, intellectual, and political liveliness of Western civilization:

> From those controversies concerning the spiritual and temporal power emerged that wealth of speculation concerning human society which made political theory so largely a western European development. The relations between the individual and society were bound to be affected by the situation, since the individual gains when instead of one master there are two who have to compete with one another for dominion over him. Even modern political liberty may be said to emerge from the politico-ecclesiastical controversies of the Middle Ages, as Lord Acton demonstrated in so many ways. More significant than this, however, was the establishment of the autonomy of the spiritual principle—the most important area of human life and activity was freed from subservience to the secular power, and the state was not presumed to

dictate to a man the moral end for which he was to live and the highest law that he should serve. Furthermore the Church—the spiritual principle in society—asserted its claim to have a voice in the arrangements of terrestrial society and the conduct of affairs, since it was concerned with the establishment of righteousness in the world. And, planted hard and firm on this earth, the Church stood there as the agency of a principle by which rulers, and secular society in general, could be judged.[6]

The great achievement of the Church in the Middle Ages, however, was its success in transforming "the more formal Christianity of the barbarians, originally mass-converted, into a profounder thing, more genuinely appropriated." Day after day, century after century, saints and missionaries preaching the Gospel throughout Europe reminded their hearers of God's love for the world and man's dignity in Christ. In the name of Christ's love they founded hospitals, universities, and orphanages. The historical consequences of this centuries-long labor of love belonged "like so many of the most important things in life and history . . . to a realm of matters so subtle that they are difficult to catch in the historian's kind of fishing-net."[7] But Butterfield had little doubt that through the patient work of its most faithful servants the Church gradually wove into the fabric of Western civilization three fundamental ideas that, to this day, even in their secularized form, give to the Western heritage much of its uniqueness.

First was the idea of a loving God who was intimately concerned with the welfare of His creation and every one of His creatures. Such intimate love implied that God's works partook of His purposefulness and His constancy. Hence, the universe was not chaotic or random, but intelligible. On the basis of this belief and its underlying world view, seventeenth-century scientists, many of whom were devout Christians, launched the enterprise of modern science that so fascinated Butterfield. A second idea was the importance of human personality, the irreducibility of a human being to anything less than a soul destined for eternity and created in God's image, the significance and meaning which the life and actions of every person contained. Finally, through the Church's work the idea of charity or unconditional love became established as the highest principle of man's moral life, as the norm by which all human actions ultimately had to be measured. The implantation of these notions in the soil of Western culture proved to be the Church's most significant earthly achievement.

Butterfield discerned a major paradox at the heart of Christianity's relation to Western civilization. Insofar as it insisted on the sacredness of the person, the intimate quality of each person's relationship with God, and the primacy of charity, Christianity paved the way for the legitimation of freedom of conscience, religious toleration, political pluralism, and a world in which Christianity no longer had a monopoly in society. The paradox worked in the face of opposition from ecclesiastical systems and Christians in power; its agency was Christian principles assimilated by unbelievers or dissenting Christians, who brandished these principles in order to dissolve the alliance between established Christianity and the state.[8] "Precisely because the medieval church did its work so well," wrote Butterfield, "it was bound to promote a kind of world that would be liable to rebel against its authority. A Christian civilization by its very nature has to develop towards what its most faithful servants feel to be its own undoing."[9]

This paradox illustrated the complex relationship within Christianity itself between the faith's spiritual dimension and its political and social aspects, between Christianity as a transcendent religion with a spiritual message and Christianity as a political and social force. It was its spiritual substance that gave Christianity its vigor, freshness, and ability to generate new developments in the world. And even when, on the basis of its spiritual reach, Christianity was able to capture the imagination and political power of an entire society, the message of the faith continued its work independent of the Christianized political institutions, often undermining their authority, pointing out their inconsistencies, and recalling them to the original Christian principles that had sprung them into life but which had lost their force during the course of the close alliance with power. Butterfield explained:

> All men in Christendom, year in and year out, for century after century, were continually being told that they were souls to be saved and that they were destined to a life eternal, . . . For those who believed this statement there could be nothing in the visible universe to which human beings could be regarded as subject or subordinate. . . . Christians and even ecclesiastical organizations might sometimes do their worst, trying all kinds of means for securing the repression of personality or organizing the dominion of man over man; but, in fact, in the course of history it always turned out sooner or later that they were hamstrung by one of their own theological dogmas which somebody or other would throw back in their faces—they were hamstrung by the very things which they were having to preach week by week about the nature of human beings and their eternal destiny.[10]

Insofar as dissenting or minority Christians, because of their exclusion from power, often acted as carriers for the prophetic indictment of established Christianity, they could serve, and in various periods of European history had served, a useful role in the continuous regeneration of Christianity. Being a Methodist himself, Butterfield had the required historical imagination to perceive this. In medieval Europe some of the monastic orders in their early inception, such as the Franciscans, had served as a focus for the rediscovery of Christian principles and a sharpening of Christian vision, in contrast to the increasing worldliness and politicization of the established ecclesiastical authorities. In Protestant England the dissenters performed a similar function; moreover, by taking a stand against the establishment they paved the ground for a reconciliation between Christianity and the modern world. Whereas in societies that had succeeded in imposing religious uniformity, such as Catholic France, Christianity was closely identified with the social, economic, and political status quo, in England the dissenters, through their involvement in movements for reform, abetted the perception of Christianity as an ally in the struggles for the rights of labor, the widening of the franchise, and the abolition of the slave trade. The essentially false contrast between Christianity and the modern world was thereby softened; political radicalism in England lacked the anti-Christian pitch of French anticlericalism; the dialogue between the Church and the political fringes of society was never cut off.

Christian principles, even against the opposition of ecclesiastical systems and many Christians, were capable of transforming the fabric of society and introducing into it strands of spiritual and social regeneration of unpredictable magnitude. The modern Western conceptions of humanism, liberalism, humanitarianism, and internationalism derived much of their original impetus from such Christian ideas as the sacredness of the person, the equality and brotherhood of all men, and the imperatives of the love ethic. Even when they later became secularized and cut off from their Christian roots, these conceptions had a humanizing influence on the quality of life in Western civilization.

Butterfield knew that the question of Christianity's role in twentieth-century international politics was a knotty one. Like Lord Acton, he had a searing consciousness of the foolishness, errors, and atrocities of which Christians in the past had been guilty when they had entered the arena of politics. During the course of the religious wars in the sixteenth and seventeenth centuries, Christianity had been a source of fanaticism, disorder, and unparalleled violence in international relations, playing a role similar to that of Nazi and Communist ideologies in our times. Lord Clarendon, a seventeenth-century English statesman much admired by Butterfield for his political judiciousness and sense of Providence and himself a staunch supporter of the Church of England, had warned that ecclesiastics were not suitable people for conducting politics or governing a country; with notable exceptions, they lacked the gifts of compromise, moderation, and the ability to put themselves in the opposite party's shoes, necessary to keep politics from degenerating into a fratricidal struggle. In the fallen world of politics, religious principles easily became screens for rigidity and intransigence, piety a cover for self-righteousness, and constancy a stepping-stone to ruthlessness. As Butterfield surmised, "a religion, and particularly a supernatural religion, can be a very dangerous thing in the world, unless accompanied by and rooted in a super-abundant charity."[11]

There were two kinds of political dangers into which Christians fell easily. One was the attempt to harness political institutions for supposedly Christian purposes. The enterprise could have constructive results if carried out for objectives so specific and limited that Christians did not face the temptation of engaging in the total transformation of society through the sheer exercise of power. The Spanish Dominicans' campaign for a more humane policy toward the conquered peoples of the New World in the sixteenth century and the efforts to abolish slavery and promote social reform on the part of nineteenth-century English dissenters were examples of beneficial Christian involvement in politics. In both cases the predominant methods had been persuasion and the moderate use of political power and the guiding image had been that of Christianity as the salt of the earth rather than a catalyst for total transformation.

Whenever Christians became overly ambitious in their political goals and undertook the wholesale capture of the City of Man in order to refashion it in the image of the City of God, the results were generally disastrous for the world and for Christianity. Neither Puritan England nor Spain at the height of the Inquisition had been models of humane, peaceful societies. As for Christianity itself, it tended to lose its integrity, to be captured by the very stubborn political realities it tried to control. It was very tempting, once Christians gained positions of authority, to sanctify the seat of power and overlook its sins, to compromise the faith's message in exchange for political breathing space. Whether one has in mind the Orthodox church's subservience to the state in tsarist Russia, or the casuistries of pro-Marxist Catholic priests in Nicaragua today, the pattern discerned by Butterfield seems to be the same.

An opposite political danger for Christians was to flee from the responsibilities of power altogether. While Christians were not obligated to participate in politics themselves, they had a duty to think responsibly about political issues and to support those leaders of the earthly city who had an accurate understanding of the human condition and of the best means to achieve relative order and harmony. The Christian simply should not wash his hands in Pilate-like fashion from the messy spectacle of power politics and retreat to the safe haven of his inner piety. As fond as he was of Acton's famous dictum, Butterfield often remarked that its obverse was also true, that the lack of power tends to corrupt, and the absolute lack of power corrupts absolutely.

Just as the approach of death, in the words of Samuel Johnson, could give a man an exceedingly clear mind, so could the exercise of power have a sobering, intellectually healthful effect upon those who undertook it. It was easy for Christians to think and act irresponsibly in political matters, and one of the best correctives could be the exercise of power or the mustering of sufficient sympathetic imagination to understand the burdensome responsibilities and dilemmas faced by those in power.

Like his much-admired Richelieu, Butterfield realized that a Christian's personal virtue was no indication of his political wisdom.[12] A good Christian was no better equipped to be a wise statesman than he was to be a skilled surgeon. The wisdom of statecraft required a sense of Providence, an awareness of the limits to power, and the gift of political forgiveness and generosity; these a Christian could hope to acquire if he derived his inspiration selectively from the finest sources in his tradition. But the wisdom of statecraft also required what Butterfield called a thorough soaking in the science of power politics, a mastery of the intricate rules of the grammar of power, an ability to make highly subtle political judgments.[13] These things, as Aristotle had taught long ago, were acquired only through long and arduous experience in the world of politics. Unfortunately, Christians rarely achieved proficiency in this latter wisdom; even when they became involved in politics, somewhere in the course of the political crucible they succumbed to the easy temptations of utopianism or self-righteousness. In international relations this meant that they relied too much on the eagerly anticipated transformation of world politics and the adversary's policies in the likeness of the Kingdom of God or else they identified their nation's cause with God's purposes in the world, shutting their eyes to whatever political realities did not correspond with this nationalistic, Messianic vision. Few Christians succeeded in combining both of the necessary aspects of the wisdom of statecraft, the broad vision of the children of light and the cunning of the children of darkness.[14]

Although Christianity occasionally could have a direct positive influence on the course of international affairs by supporting or condemning particular policies or by inspiring the imaginative statesmanship of some Christians, its most significant contribution, according to Butterfield, was "in providing the proper background of ideas or the spirit with which to set to work" in the conduct of foreign policy.[15] Christian theology, for example, could help citizens and politicians alike to straighten out their ideas on human sin, reminding them that in international politics, "though extraordinary criminals do exist, the really knotty problem is that of human nature generally," in particular "the moderate cupidities" of one's own countrymen which can put great pressure on the nation's foreign policy.[16]

Also, at the twin levels of policymaking and public opinion, Christianity could temper the evils of excessive fear and overanxiety, evils which Butterfield counted as among "the great sources of political error and miscalculation" and "one of the gravest threats to young and inexperienced democracies." [17] The biblical counsel, "Fret not thyself because of evildoers," had major political implications. As Butterfield interpreted it, this admonition "does not mean that you must never try to right a wrong but . . . it explicitly intends to remind you that you must not expect to win every time, you must not say that you will make no peace with Heaven until all evils are eradicated." [18] By challenging the intellectual arrogance and passionate self-love of Everyman and fostering the virtue of humility within a society's political and cultural climate, Christianity in its finest moments could check what Butterfield called the recurrent tendency of the people and its leaders to direct the course of international relations "by the might of a sovereign will, achieving one's object by too great an exercise of power." [19]

Butterfield also thought that certain strains of Christian thought had served in the past as a fertile subsoil for the kind of moderate political realism he prized in the conduct of statecraft. Christian notions of universal sin had contributed to the development of the theory of the balance of power by Fénelon and others. A Christian awareness of the need to reconcile divergent interests among states had aided in the growth of the institutions of international diplomacy, as had also notions of Providence. And, in the hands of Vitoria, Grotius, and their successors, Christian concerns for the normative dimensions of politics had been inseparable from the development of international law and the idea of an international order held together by common rules and principles of conduct. Perhaps in the future Christian principles would play a similar role by indirectly helping to shape politically sound forms of statecraft.

The continuing decline of Christianity's political and cultural predominance in the West carried grave dangers, but it also presented promising opportunities. On the one hand the loss of the Church's moral authority meant the weakening of a powerful barrier to the dehumanizing forces latent in the materialistic, technological society of the late twentieth century. This was an even more worrisome development when one considered that the great secularized derivations of Christianity that had contributed to the West's distinctive cultural, moral, and political order—the respect for human personality and the individualization of compassion—were also losing their vigor.

Yet, unlike some of his more pessimistic Christian contemporaries, Butterfield thought that the twentieth century also offered to Christianity unparalleled possibilities for growth and for making its mark in a world well aware of its own brokenness and limitations. Now that custom, the social consensus, and the power of the state were no longer allied with it, Christianity had to go back to its essentials, to the great themes with which it had once captured the human imagination, the themes of universal sin, forgiveness, and redemption which in the light of the apocalyptic realities of contemporary international politics were more relevant than they had seemed a century or two ago. Deprived of its role as the bond of the tribe, Christianity had to address itself again to the conscience of every person, thereby recovering its authenticity and spiritual integrity.

Christians, therefore, were not to despair over the passing of Christendom, nor were they to hold on to its remaining fragments with all their might against the opposition of the world. The true image, etched throughout the Gospel itself, was that of dying in order to live, giving in order to receive. The great culture of the West—its music and art, its universities, its finest ideals—had been to a considerable measure a gift of the Church to the world. There were other, newer opportunities for Christians to make another gift to the world, to spread the Gospel and derive rich implications from it in politics and culture. As the West fully worked out the consequences of its secular humanism, Christianity might appear again as it did to the civilization of late Rome, a bright light in the midst of man's great tragedy. Meanwhile, throughout the developing world Christianity—insofar as it was perceived less and less as an arm of the West's culture and power—had exciting prospects as it offered a fresh alternative to both Western secular individualism and collectivist atheist Marxism.

Butterfield's emphasis on the relevance of Christianity for the modern world and the Christian orientation of his own political philosophy raise an important question. To what extent are Butterfield's ideas valid or even useful for non-Christian peoples in today's multicultural international society? This is the question posed by some political scientists with regard to Butterfield's work. Before an answer can be sketched it is necessary to make some preliminary observations. It is impossible to ground any prescriptive counsels in political science on purely scientific, objective, or universal grounds. Whenever the political scientist goes beyond description and enters the realm of prescription, he necessarily enters the realm of values. His choice of values, in turn, rests on processes and assumptions that are always far from being either scientific, in the sense of being subject to universal verification, objective, in the sense of being separable from the subjective preferences of his self and the forces of environment and accidental circumstances that have helped to shape that self and its inner direction, or universal, in the sense of being readily acceptable to peoples of different cultures and different historical periods.

Therefore, the criticism aimed at Butterfield is no different from that which could be aimed at any political scientist who advocates a particular set of policies and in support of them offers a selective list of values and value derivations. Upon close scrutiny, all such proposals, no matter how supposedly scientific and universal their foundation, will be discovered to rest on subjective preferences for values that are not universal. During the last two decades, many Western specialists in the field of international relations have agonized over this problem. They have sought to construct a universally valid normative foundation from which they can derive policies that can be acceptable to all of the world's peoples and cultures.[20] The enterprise has been encouraged by the belief that Western political science has been too Western in its orientation, and that it needs to shed its subjectivity in exchange for a universal perspective fitting for a multicultural world. Because of the impossibility of transcending human subjectivity, these efforts have failed, and the results have fallen short of the initial expectations. Inevitably, whether in the case of Lasswell-McDougal or that of Falk-Mendlovitz, the values offered as an analytical foundation have been short of universal and have reflected instead the peculiar orientations of their proponents (a twentieth-century version of classical individualist liberalism combined with a subtle but tenacious faith in progress and modern science, as in McDougal's case; or a neo-Marxist, solidarist humanism, as with Falk and Mendlovitz). Although sometimes the values, such as McDougal's choice of freedom, human dignity, and world order, will appear deceptively universal, their application in today's world, as Adda Bozemen has pointed out, is likely to produce highly divergent interpretations and applications of them in accordance with the cultural and political soil on which they are planted.

Herbert Butterfield, to paraphrase Adam Watson, was a Christian without chauvinism but also without regrets. Deeply aware though he was of the abuses and wrongs committed by Christians in power (many of them, indeed, against the peoples of the Third World), he did not embark on a wholesale rejection of his heritage. He believed that Christianity had much to offer to the entire world. For him, the contemporary multicultural international society, with its advancing industrial civilization, its refined skepticism, and its moral and religious relativism was analogous to the civilization of the Roman Empire in which Christianity first set its roots. Moreover, what he liked to call the recurring dilemmas and predicaments of human existence had not been altered radically in the course of two millennia. Thus, Christ's message was highly relevant today, even if its implications might be worked out in forms culturally and intellectually different from those of the past, in view of the sharply different circumstances of the present world.

Instead of claiming for Christianity or his interpretations of it a false universality or scientific character, Butterfield simply challenged his generation to evaluate it as all normative foundations must be evaluated, not through some supposedly scientific process but in the light of human experience, the constellation of circumstances known as the human condition, moral reasoning, and by comparison with alternative modes of normative action. In this respect, Christianity had no fewer claims to transcultural validity than any of the normative models proposed by twentieth-century political science.

Butterfield's favorite images of Christianity's interaction with civilization were the salt of the earth and the leaven that leavens the whole bread. Both of these conveyed a sense of the elusiveness with which Christianity could effect its transformations in society whenever it operated through the imagination and moral energies of human beings rather than through the raw power of political or social coercion. That these transformations, at once elusive and concrete, unpredictable and purposeful, would continue throughout the future, leavening the substance of world history, Butterfield had no doubt. As he warned, with reference to Christianity, "spiritual forces have an extraordinary spontaneity and originality so that we can never tell what a man may not do when he says to himself 'How shall I worship God?,' and we can never tell what he may not do just for love."[21] In another important respect, therefore, Christianity was likely to leave its imprint on the course of world politics. In the aftermath of the numerous conflicts that would continue to punctuate international relations in the late twentieth century and beyond, in the midst of the wreckage recurrently left by nations in their furious struggle for survival and power, Christianity with its Word and works of unconditional charity, hope, and reconciliation would help to give substance and meaning to the efforts of statesmen to bring order out of chaos and life out of destruction.

V

The Wisdom of Statecraft

For we know that the whole creation groaneth and travaileth in pain together until now. And not only they, but ourselves also, who have the first fruits of the Spirit, even we ourselves groan within ourselves, waiting for the adoption, that is, the redemption of our body. For we are saved by hope. But hope that is seen is not hope; for what a man seeth, why doth he yet hope for? But if we hope for that which we see not, then do we with patience wait for it.

Romans 8 : 22 − 25

9

Butterfield and the quest
for political wisdom
in international relations

Before summarizing Butterfield's most important contribu-
tions to international political theory, it is necessary to deal with two major
questions posed by his work that are highly relevant to the issue of the political usefulness of his insights. The first question is that of the role of the individual in history. From ancient times to the present, historians, philosophers, and writers such as Thucydides, Machiavelli, Jacob Burckhardt, Karl
Marx, and Leo Tolstoy have inquired into the relationship between conditioning circumstances, necessity, and the larger forces underlying the historical process and the impact of great personalities and towering individuals on
the course of human events.[1] The more deterministically one views history
and politics and the greater weight one gives to the first set of factors, the less
inclined one is to think that the kind of philosophy of statecraft outlined by
Butterfield is of any practical importance. If, on the other hand, one be-
lieves—as did Thucydides, Machiavelli, Burckhardt, and Butterfield—
that, in spite of the major role of conditioning circumstances and forces beyond the control of any single individual, human beings can and often do
make an important difference in the turns that history takes, then a wisdom
of statecraft can be of significant value to statesmen and to the world in which
they live.

Butterfield's debate with Marxist historiography and the school of Sir
Lewis Namier, as well as his commentaries on Acton and Ranke, revealed a
sophisticated understanding of the role of the individual in history. This understanding was grounded on an awareness of both the power and creativity
of human personality and the influence which larger economic, social, and
intellectual currents play in conditioning, limiting, and channelling human
action. Concerning the first dimension, Butterfield insisted:

The genesis of historical events lies in human beings. The real birth of ideas takes place in human brains. The reason why things happen is that human beings have vitality. From the historian's point of view it is this that makes the world go round. If we take all the individuals of France at a given moment in 1789, they represent what in one respect can be regarded as so many separate wells of life, so many sources of decision and action. . . . if we start imagining that the French Revolution stood up and did something as though it were a self-acting agent (when we really mean that a certain man or group of men came to some decision or other) . . . then we are moving into a world of optical illusions. . . . Economic factors, financial situations, wars, political crises, do not cause anything, do not do anything, do not exist except as abstract terms and convenient pieces of shorthand. . . . It is men who make history.[2]

Butterfield never wanted to lose sight of the centrality of the individual in the historical process. Moreover, as a Methodist and a historian he was impressed by the rich particularities of historical events and personalities, he believed that individuals had a degree of free will, a number of genuine choices open to them. It was for these reasons that he so vigorously emphasized the importance of narrative history and, in works as thematically different as *The Peace Tactics of Napoleon* and *The Origins of Modern Science*, his historical analysis developed as a story in which the thoughts and decisions of the actors made a difference in the course of events, sometimes with incalculable consequences for future generations. As he explained:

There is something in history to which we can do justice only by reproducing the course of events as a story, the kind of story in which we do not know what is going to happen next. And most of us are aware in fact that the understanding of the past may be obstructed if the student has been unable to unload from his mind the foreknowledge that he possesses, his awareness of how the story is going to end. When the narrative is allowed to present itself in hard lines, giving an impression of rigid inevitability, such an effect is calculated to make us sceptical of the possibility of altering the world by any action of ours. It is important, therefore, to remember that the effect is a trick of the historian's mirror; for there is no irrevocability in human action except that which is the equivalent of the statement that the action has already been performed.[3]

This awareness of the fluidity of history had important implications for Butterfield's political thinking. The course of international politics was for him to some extent a drama in which one could not be quite sure what would happen next. Butterfield believed that in the conduct of foreign affairs the statesman should see the alignments and balances of political forces as constantly changing and the broad trends of international politics not as predetermined or inevitable but as subject to alteration, given the passage of time and the exercise of patience and skill on the part of the statesman. Change was one of the perennial motifs in the history of international relations, and statesmen who eschewed a deterministic view of history and politics could take advantage of the fluidity created by change to achieve their objectives. In other words, the state of flux, which with varying degrees of intensity characterized much of the course of international relations, provided the individual statesman with recurrent opportunities to leave his mark on history, to rise above the larger forces and trends and perhaps make his own authentic contribution to the destiny of his people and—in the case of a few extraordinary individuals—the world.

Individuals also played an important role in history at the level of their private, as distinct from their public, lives. Drawing on the ideas of the French philosopher Henri Bergson and the Scottish essayist and historian Thomas Carlyle, Butterfield underscored the importance of personal virtue, or the lack of it, when multiplied by millions of members of society:

> Wars may be caused, or empires fall, or civilizations decline, not necessarily through some colossal criminality in the first place, but from multitudinous cases of petty betrayal or individual neglect. . . . all of us must be able to recall occasions when our doing a trifle more or a trifle less than our duty has had a magnified effect which we should never have calculated. Not only do little things become magnified, but big things, like our victory in the Second World War, sometimes appear to be achieved by so small a margin that we hold our breath at the memory of the hairbreadth escape.[4]

In the tradition of classical political science, Butterfield was unable to divorce private from public virtue entirely. These two forms of virtue were different from one another, and it was possible, as David Hume pointed out, to discover instances in which private virtue could accompany public vice and public virtue be joined to private vice. Nevertheless, at the level of the entire community the nurture of individual virtue was necessary to sustain public virtue, and no sound political order could endure without having as a foundation a large number of individuals who in their daily lives quietly and unostentatiously went about faithfully carrying out their public and private duties. Butterfield worried that in modern democratic societies, with their large populations clustered in cities that fostered a pervasive sense of anonymity and alienation, it was easy for many individuals to come to believe that their actions were of little consequence and to neglect those seemingly small duties and acts of virtue indispensable to the well-being of the whole.[5]

In addition to the creative statesman or great historical figure and the ordinary human beings who in their totality shaped the character of a society, Butterfield singled out what he called "the cell" as an important mode by which individuals could have a decisive impact on the course of history. Developments of great significance "could be produced through the conscious purpose of twenty men, none of them possessing artificial advantages at the beginning of the story—twenty men united by a sense of mission." Such small groups or "cells" had numerous advantages. As Butterfield put it, a cell

> is a remorseless self-multiplier; it is exceptionally difficult to destroy; it can preserve its intensity of local life while vast organizations quickly wither when they are weakened at the centre; it can defy the power of governments; and it is the appropriate level for prising open any *status quo*. Whether we take early Christianity or sixteenth-century Calvinism or the French revolutionary period or modern communism, this seems the appointed way by which a mere handful of people may open a new chapter in the history of civilization. And the men who form cells are pursuing a higher strategy than those who seek immediately to capture governments; for those who make a direct bid to capture a government must bow before existing gods and existing tendencies in order to open a path to power; while those who form cells have no need to dilute their purposes or to purchase favour from the supporters of the *status quo*.[6]

Concerned though he was with highlighting the meaning and wide scope of individual action, Butterfield was quick to admit that few people "would challenge the ascription of a considerable area of human life to law and necessity." Indeed, "the margin that we may leave for choices made by individuals in conditions under which some other choice is presumed to have been possible for them is like a small segment cut out of the great circle of necessity."[7] The problem with much Marxist thought, as with many of the historical studies of the Namier school, was not that it emphasized the role of economic forces and motives but that it neglected noneconomic circumstances affecting individual behavior such as political ideals, religion, and notions of honor and virtue. Marxism also implicitly denied the authenticity of individual freedom and the possibility of even partly transcending the limitations imposed on the human spirit by the larger economic and social forces at work in the historical moment. For Butterfield, the truly great historians were those such as Ranke and Acton who were able to incorporate both aspects of history, freedom and necessity, the irreducible element of spontaneity in every human personality and the pressing forces and circumstances limiting such spontaneity, into what he considered "a higher synthesis" of historical and political analysis.[8]

One of the paradoxes inherent in the relationship of freedom and necessity was that, by recognizing the scope of necessity in history, an individual could manage and redirect for his own purposes forces and circumstances that otherwise would have crushed him, thus asserting his freedom in the end. "By diagnosing and recognizing where he is unfree, man may increase his power and steal a march on the whole system of necessity." Whatever laws may exist in history can be "superseded by the mere fact that men have become conscious of them" and have proceeded "to take special measures to counteract" them.[9] A greater knowledge of the continuities and recurrent patterns of history did not need to lead to fatalism or a sense of personal helplessness, but could provide an opportunity for man's creative exercise of his freedom and initiative. For instance, America's Founding Fathers at the conclusion of the War of Independence and the English Whigs of the eighteenth and nineteenth centuries knew, from their acquaintance with the English Civil War, the tendency of revolutions to veer ever leftwards and destroy every font of order and moderation in a society. They used that knowledge to direct successfully their aspirations for political change within the channels of orderly reform. Similarly, in the late twentieth century a statesman could contemplate realistically the tendencies of international politics towards recurrent anarchy and violence and then use that knowledge as a foundation on which to build a durable international order by means of mechanisms such as the balance of power and diplomacy which had as their objectives not the abolition but the redirection of such tendencies towards constructive purposes.

Like Jacob Burckhardt and Leopold von Ranke, Butterfield was fascinated with the role of great men in history.[10] In his stirring eulogy on the death of Sir Winston Spencer Churchill, given before a packed Great Saint Mary's Church at Cambridge, he outlined some of the qualities that defined a great leader in a democratic society. Churchill was "unusually conscious" of where he and his generation stood "in the march of history." During the great crisis of 1940–45, he had been "more sensitive than others to the fact that here was a historic moment," and that "one must behave as though already under the eye of generations still unborn." Through his historical awareness and poetic imagination, Churchill quickly grasped that the war was more than a mundane power play amenable to easy resolution; instead, the destiny of his people and an entire civilization were at stake, and nothing less than an epic summoning of all the moral and intellectual resources within the statesman and his people would suffice. Churchill's response to the relentless advance of England's foes was a "magnificent assertion of the human will" which belied the notion of historical inevitability.[11]

The "interior richness" of Churchill's personality was complemented by "a superintending mind, capable of communicating energy to all the parts of the governmental machine, and prepared for super-human labour." Even more important was "the special relationship that Churchill established with the nation as a whole." His mind's "ample command of colour" and his rhetorical skills were the intangibles through which he established that relationship. In his conduct of public affairs, Churchill was not a slave to public opinion and its passions. In a style reminiscent of the Burkean tradition of political representation, he often disagreed with the majority and even attempted to challenge and educate it. As Butterfield explained:

> Public opinion in itself often stands in an amorphous state, mixed with a million little egotisms—not always simply to be humored or passively followed, because multitudes of individuals can think or say or shout a lot of things, to which they will not necessarily commit their souls if pressed. Churchill pressed them knowing that, when men are challenged and roused, they are capable of making a high response—capable even of being grateful to the leader who gave them a shaking-up. And if he and public opinion sometimes did not agree at the finish, it was like two great powers confronting one another, each with a remarkable respect for the other.[12]

There was another characteristic which helped to account for the human warmth in Churchill's relationship with the British people. He was a tough and determined politician, yet he also was able to "set an example of the sort of tolerances and urbanities which are necessary for the conduct of democracy—that respect for the other man's personality without which democracy will crumble into a chaos of egotisms." Butterfield's eulogy was not a complete portrait of his feelings about Churchill. During World War II, for example, the great historian had been disappointed and upset by Churchill's policy of "unconditional surrender" and his refusal to show towards Germany some of that far-sighted magnanimity of which he was sometimes capable in domestic affairs. Nevertheless, Butterfield thought that on the whole Churchill had three of the most valuable qualities for the statesman of a democratic society: a deep awareness of history and of the significance of the historical moment in which he lived; an ability to lead his people by drawing on the resources of a rich imagination, political oratory, great ideas, and a strong, determined personality; and a sense of toleration, the perception that for the most part one's adversaries, outside and within, partake of our common humanity.

A second major question posed by Butterfield's work is that of whether man actually learns anything from history. This was the subject of the 1971 Rede Lecture he gave at Cambridge University, which was aptly entitled, "The Discontinuities between the Generations in History: Their Effect on the Transmission of Political Experience." He set out to inquire "whether, in those regions where comparison is feasible, we go on making the same mistakes in human relations, or at least in the things that concern the internal and external relations of states, as were made by the earliest civilisations." He thought that the concept of a generation and the kind of transition that often takes place in the mental outlook of an entire society as a generation succeeds another was pivotal in understanding the degree to which man succeeded or failed in profiting from his predecessors' political experience. Some of Butterfield's contemporaries, including the Spanish philosopher José Ortega y Gasset and the American political theorist Lewis Feuer also had explored this theme of the generation and its impact on political life, although from disciplines other than history.[13]

It was difficult for historical science to explain or describe with complete exactitude the precise changes that sometimes occurred in the transition from one generation to another. Nevertheless, such changes took place, and they involved an entirely new way of seeing things, a transformed universe of thought and discourse in which new assumptions, new categories, and new paradigms replaced older ones, sometimes with hardly a stir or a conscious recognition that such a radical change had just occurred. This was the problem with which, on a large scale, C. S. Lewis had grappled in *The Discarded Image*, on the transition from the medieval to the modern mind. Butterfield saw an illustration in the Scientific Revolution of the seventeenth century and the drastic changes in man's perceptions of the universe and the earth's place in it. At the even smaller scale of a single generation, Butterfield saw several examples of the subtlety and profound significance of the discontinuities and transitions generated by the passage from one generation to another. There was, for example, the successor generation to the English Civil War which, in contradistinction to its forebears and largely because of the latter's painful experience with revolution and violence, developed the philosophy and practice of political compromise and moderation for which the Whigs later became renowned. There was also the change in British attitudes towards the American colonies on the part of a group of younger men around 1760, who, against the wiser counsels of some of their elders, thought that Great Britain had been far too lenient and pusillanimous towards the colonies and should tax and regulate them more extensively. One also could detect an equally subtle and significant change in the attitudes of major European statesmen between, for example, the Bismarck generation of 1870 and its successor generation that was involved in the outbreak of World War I in

1914. At some point in the transition from one generation to another, the sense of prudence and common responsibility for the international order had been either lost or superseded by narrowed definitions of the national interest. The men of 1914, as Henry Kissinger has put it, had lost the sense of tragedy, the awareness of the precariousness of international order which their predecessors only a few decades before still had.

The transition of the generations thus could have salutary or harmful political consequences, although it was difficult for a historian to explain why, in a particular instance, a new generation sought to elaborate and cultivate the wisdom of the past, while in another it rejected it as useless or noxious. In cases such as the development of the Whig tradition of the eighteenth century or the elaboration from Richelieu to Bismarck of a tradition of prudent statecraft based on the careful management of the balance of power, successive generations had sought to learn from the political experience of the past and applied such knowledge to contemporary problems. In other instances, however, a successor generation became impatient with, or perhaps grew tired of, the received tradition and proceeded to discard that entire tradition, including its most valuable insights.

In Rankean fashion, Butterfield concluded that the future course of history would witness similar zigzags and cycles in man's ability and desire to improve his condition by learning from the mistakes of the past. Occasionally it would prove possible to develop a long-lasting political tradition, in either domestic or foreign policy, that would incorporate the wisdom of the past in addressing the challenges of the present. But such traditions were not immune to either gradual disintegration, as successive generations forgot the urgency and value of the tradition's message, or to sudden collapse under a massive assault at the hands of an impatient or apocalyptic-minded generation. The breakdown of a tradition would be followed by a period of chaos and political disorder of indeterminate duration. This eventually might lead to the gradual emergence of a new tradition incorporating portions of the old if a generation came along which thought it useful to bring to the chaos of the present an element of order out of the experiences of the past. Clearly, there was no guarantee of uniform progress in history, no guarantee of man being able to draw on his collective historical memory and political experience to reduce progressively the number and scope of political problems until he reaches the point of absolute mastery over them. The clue to such impossibility was the generation. And while the generation might be seen as a curse, in the sense that it made indefinite progress impossible, it was also, in Butterfield's eyes, a blessing in the form of a guarantee of man's freedom. No generation could imprison completely its successors within its own ideals and institutions; every generation was free to alter these, discarding and replacing them or improving upon them.

The implications of Butterfield's observations for political science are clear. Although theoretically it may be possible to gain cumulative knowledge of political problems, this does not mean that political science will enable man some day to solve conclusively those problems. Man applies knowledge to the solution of problems through value choices and through essentially subjective interpretations and evaluations of the significance of the available knowledge. Insofar as a generation may make value choices or interpretations different from those of its predecessors, there will never be definitive solutions to the dilemmas of politics, only endless experimentation and adaptations suited to the full range of diversity of human values and circumstances and to man's quest for the fulfillment of his tragic freedom.[14] The same is true, of course, of historical science and, implicitly, of Butterfield's own work. While it is possible to learn some lessons from history and apply these to the political realm, the enterprise is not likely to lift man out of the essentially tragic predicaments of the human condition.

Seizing on the observations of writers and historians such as St. Augustine, Orosius, Otto of Freising, and Machiavelli, Butterfield emphasized the difficulty encountered by any historian who tries to impress his readers with the sufferings and calamities of bygone generations. Even the most eloquent accounts of the misery of others hardly touch us, especially when they concern people separated from us by time or distance. Thus it seems that, for the most part, the noble efforts of gifted historians notwithstanding, almost every generation has to make its own mistakes, has to experience its sorrows and pain and taste in its own palate the bitter fruits of human foolishness and presumptuousness. Apart from the problem of the diversity of human events, which makes it inappropriate to apply mechanically to one historical moment the lessons derived from another, there are severe limits to the transmission of political experience.

Throughout Butterfield's writings there emerge three different sources of wisdom for the statesman in the conduct of foreign policy: history, political theory and practice, and the Christian tradition. History could enrich the statesman's ability to make sound political judgments in at least two ways. The first was through its methods; by cultivating the best qualities of the historical mind, the skills of intellectual understanding and sympathetic imagination, and applying these to the issues of international relations, the statesman might broaden the range of considerations on which he based his decisions. This was of great importance, since the pressures of national self-righteousness and the average man's cupidity and desire for national glory tended to restrict the statesman's perspective dangerously.

Butterfield thought that a statesman never could have too much understanding or too strong a capacity to put himself in the position of others.

Obviously a statesman differed from the academic historian in that he could not allow his catholicity of thought to paralyze him; his ability to see the world as the other party saw it had to be translated into the service of his country's best interests.[15] Understanding, therefore, did not mean appeasement. It meant seeing political reality as the adversary or ally saw it, without either exaggerating or downplaying his strengths, his predicaments, or his fears. Such perception could only help the statesman in fashioning a prudent and realistic foreign policy. By suggesting ways in which the qualities and underlying attitudes of the historical mind could be transposed to the realm of political decisions, Butterfield rendered an important service to both political science and practical statecraft.

A second aspect of history's contribution to political wisdom was the substance of history itself; through the study of the past, a statesman could expand the frontiers of his necessarily narrow political experience. The limitations of time and place and the distortions of short-term political pressures might be lessened if the statesman could place his work in the context of the march of several generations and of a wider world extending beyond his state's borders. The past was not a source of ready-made lessons for the present but a vast canvas on which the statesman could appreciate the limits and possibilities of statecraft and thus gain a more accurate measure of his own limits and possibilities. In Butterfield's words,

> It is of considerable advantage to acquire one's basic knowledge of politics from distant examples, where the controversy is over, the story completed, the passion spent. By this method, one gains a notion of the structure of political conflict which one can never gain in the fever of one's own contemporary world. Then, when one returns to the present, one is able to see it more analytically. The alternative rather seduces one into carrying present-day passions into the past. Those who want to learn the anatomy of international warfare had better begin with something as dead as the War of Troy. Even the study of long periods and distant ranges of history may be important, producing a more flexible understanding of politics than short periods or recent events.[16]

Over the long span of many centuries continuities and changes, the recurrent and the novel were so intertwined that, even if he profited in no other way from the study of the past, the statesman was well served by gaining an awareness of the sheer unpredictability, the innumerable surprises, with which the course of human events was filled. He then would be less likely to succumb to either of two common political fallacies: the belief that things will go on as before or the alternate view that all is in flux and there is nothing to be learned from previous generations. The study of history could

sharpen the statesman's political vision by helping him to distinguish continuities from novelties.[17] It could give him that "elasticity of mind" integral
to prudence. According to Butterfield:

> If a man had a knowledge of many wars and of the whole history
> of the art of war, studying not merely the accounts of battles and
> campaigns, but relating the weapons of a given period to the con-
> ditions of the time, relating policies to circumstances, so that he
> came to have an insight into the deep causes of things, the hidden
> sources of the changes that take place—if he allowed this knowl-
> edge not to lie heavily on his mind, not to be used in a narrow and
> literal spirit, but to sink into the walls of his brain so that it was
> turned into wisdom and experience—then such a person would be
> able to acquire the right feeling for the texture of events, and
> would undoubtedly avoid becoming the mere slave of the past. I
> think he would be better able to face a new world, and to meet the
> surprises of unpredictable change with greater flexibility. A little
> history may make people mentally rigid. Only if we go on learn-
> ing more and more of it—go on "unlearning" it—will it correct
> its own deficiencies gradually and help us to reach the required
> elasticity of mind.[18]

Political theory and practice were two other major elements of the
wisdom of statecraft. Butterfield's political theory began with the assumption
of the tragic character of human existence. Such tragedy, in turn, affected the
course of international politics. Michael Howard's description of Martin
Wight is applicable to Butterfield himself, whose outlook was in many respects similar to that of his friend Wight. "For him, International Relations
did not consist of a succession of problems to be solved in conformity with
any overarching theory. Rather, like the whole of human life, it was a predicament: one to be intelligently analysed, where possible to be mitigated,
but if necessary to be endured—and the more easily mitigated and endured
if it could be understood."[19]

The awareness of tragedy might set limits to the statesman's hubris, as
might also an understanding of Providence and of the moral judgment seemingly at work in the historical process. Though neither Providence nor judgment had a pattern fully discernible to the statesman's eye, they both were
expressions of the moral and political obligations of statecraft to recognize its
ethical boundaries and material limitations and to fashion a foreign policy in
keeping with these.

Political wisdom also consisted of recognizing the ubiquity of power in
international relations, the inescapable impact which power had on the behavior of states and on the will and perceptions of the statesman. A large

dimension of international politics was power politics. Therefore, only institutions whose methods and underlying assumptions implied a recognition of the realities of power could be effective in channelling the most destructive features of power politics in a more civilized direction. Among the institutions most capable of this difficult task, Butterfield singled out the balance of power, diplomacy, and that elusive set of norms and practices embodied in his conception of an international order. Despite the massive changes in the dynamics of world politics since 1914, Butterfield thought that these institutions still retained much of their usefulness and vigor, especially by comparison with the numerous substitutes proposed by their critics.

The political realism of the wisdom of statecraft could be complemented by the wisdom of Christianity. The Christian emphasis on the universality of sin was a major barrier against both self-righteousness and the recurring temptation to ignore the tragic dimensions of international politics. The Christian view of the human condition could be a powerful antidote to utopianism.

At the same time, by uncompromisingly affirming the sacredness of human personality, Christianity provided the statesman with a much needed, even if frequently neglected, anchor in the ground of normative imperatives. Even while assiduously studying and following the rules of the grammar of power, the statesman should not forget the elementary reason for being of the intricate political and military machinery at his disposal: the achievement of conditions of relative order and stability conducive to the pursuit of the good life by the many individual human beings under his authority. In Butterfield's thought, as in Richelieu's, reason of state had a strong normative foundation.

Christianity made its contribution to the wisdom of statecraft not only by affecting directly the statesman's attitudes but also, and perhaps most importantly, by indirectly coloring the overall moral and political outlook of society. This latter influence could be of vital significance in democracies, where the formation of foreign policy was so much at the mercy of public opinion and the respectable passions of Everyman. The relationship of Christianity to political wisdom was not free of ambiguities, of course. Butterfield's own renunciation of prudence in his advocacy of unilateral nuclear disarmament pointed to the problems that could arise whenever the delicate tension between the principles of the City of God and those of the City of Man was dissolved into a crude transcendentalism which, despite its moral passion, was immoral in its disregard for consequences.

It was thus important for Christianity, if it hoped to have a voice in the elaboration of political wisdom, to shy away from the traditions of earthly Messianism that were a part of its heritage and instead affirm a different perspective that was even more central to its world view, the Pauline reminder that even though "the whole creation groaneth and travaileth in pain," it continues to await the day of its redemption which is beyond man's power to bring. The implications of this Christian vision of reality were discernible in Butterfield's counsels to the statesman, despite what he said on the nuclear issue. The elimination of the tragic character of international politics and the resolution of its perpetual moral and political dilemmas through some transcendent principle or ideology were beyond the statesman's realm of action. To recognize this and act accordingly was, indeed, the beginning of the wisdom of statecraft.

Notes

1 Sir Herbert Butterfield: The historian, the political thinker, and the Christian

1. For a general discussion of Butterfield's life and works, see the introductory chapter in *Herbert Butterfield: Writings on Christianity and History*, ed. C. T. McIntire (New York: Oxford University Press, 1979), pp. xi–lvii. Kenneth W. Thompson, *Masters of International Thought* (Baton Rouge: Louisiana State University Press, 1980), 5–17, offers a biographical account of Butterfield while discussing the salient themes of his writings. Another rendering is found in Maurice Cowling, "Herbert Butterfield: 1900–1979," in *Proceedings of the British Academy*, vol. 65 (1979) (London: Oxford University Press, 1981), 595–609. See also the memorial address by Professor Owen Chadwick and comments by Brian Wormald in "Obituaries: Sir Herbert Butterfield," *The Cambridge Review* (November 16, 1979), 6–9; and Patrick Cosgrave, "An Englishman and His History," *Spectator*, vol. 243 (July 28, 1979), 22–23. For a complete bibliography of Butterfield's works up to 1968, see the listing by R. W. K. Hinton in the *Diversity of History: Essays in Honor of Herbert Butterfield*, ed. J. H. Elliott and H. G. Koenigsberger (London: Routledge and Kegan Paul, 1970), 315–25.
2. Herbert Butterfield, *The Origins of History* (New York: Basic Books, 1981), 180–84; "Comments on Hedley Bull's Paper on the Grotian Conception of International Relations" (unpublished paper presented at meeting of the British Committee on the Theory of International Politics, 20–23 July 1962).
3. Chadwick, "Obituaries: Sir Herbert Butterfield," 7.
4. McIntire, *Herbert Butterfield: Writings on Christianity and History*, xx–xxi.
5. Kenneth W. Thompson, ed., *Herbert Butterfield: The Ethics of History and Politics* (Washington, D.C.: University Press of America, 1980), 50.
6. Chadwick, "Obituaries: Sir Herbert Butterfield," 8.
7. Ibid., 7.
8. McIntire, *Herbert Butterfield: Writings on Christianity and History*, xii.
9. Ibid.
10. Herbert Butterfield, *Man on His Past* (Cambridge, Eng.: Cambridge University Press, 1955), 26–31.

2 The origins of history

1. Butterfield, *Origins of History*, 14.
2. Ibid., 15.
3. Ibid., 29–35, 202.
4. Ibid., 41.

5. Ibid., 62–63.
6. Ibid., 65.
7. Ibid., 80–81.
8. Ibid., 88.
9. For a useful discussion of the theme of Providence and its role in Western historiography, see Karl Löwith, *Meaning in History* (Chicago: University of Chicago Press, 1949).
10. Butterfield, *Origins of History*, 114.
11. Ibid.
12. Ibid., 137.
13. Ibid., 141.
14. Herbert Butterfield, *Christianity and History* (New York: Scribner's, 1950), 7.
15. Butterfield, *Origins of History*, 146–52.
16. Ibid., 152–53.
17. Ibid., 152–55.
18. Cited in Kenneth W. Thompson, *Morality and Foreign Policy* (Baton Rouge: Louisiana State University Press, 1980), 75.
19. Butterfield, *Origins of History*, 171.
20. Ibid., 179–80.
21. Ibid., 182.
22. Ibid., 196–97.
23. Lord Acton, "Ranke," *The Chronicle* (London) (July 20, 1867), 393–95, cited in Butterfield, *Man on His Past*, 229.
24. Butterfield, *Origins of History*, 198.
25. Ibid., 210.
26. Ibid., 220.
27. Butterfield, *Christianity and History*, 146.
28. Butterfield, *Man on His Past*, 31.

3   The mind of the historian

1. Cowling, "Herbert Butterfield," 595.
2. Butterfield, *Man on His Past*, 30.
3. Ibid., 26–27.
4. Ibid., 27.
5. Ibid.
6. Ibid.
7. Ibid., 28–29. See Hans Kohn, ed., *German History: Some New German Views* (London: Allen & Unwin, 1954).
8. Butterfield, *Man on His Past*, 23.
9. Butterfield, *Christianity and History*, 14.
10. Owen Chadwick, "Obituaries: Sir Herbert Butterfield," *The Cambridge Review* (November 16, 1979), 7.
11. Herbert Butterfield, *The Peace Tactics of Napoleon, 1806–1808* (Cambridge, Eng.: Cambridge University Press, 1929), 231–32.
12. Herbert Butterfield, *The Whig Interpretation of History* (New York: Norton, 1965), 15.
13. Ibid., 16–17.
14. Ibid., 18.
15. Ibid., 21; Butterfield, *Christianity and History*, 38–39.
16. Butterfield, *The Whig Interpretation*, 47.
17. Ibid., 42.
18. Ibid., 46–47.

19. Ibid., 28.
20. Ibid., 36–49, 28.
21. Ibid., 38, 63.
22. For a development of this theme, see Herbert Butterfield, *The Discontinuities between the Generations in History*, Rede Lecture, 1971 (London: Cambridge University Press, 1972).
23. Butterfield, *The Whig Interpretation*, 65.
24. Herbert Butterfield, "Morality and an International Order," in *The Aberystwyth Papers: International Politics, 1919–1969*, edited by Brian Porter (London: Oxford University Press, 1972), 343.
25. Butterfield, *The Whig Interpretation*, 114.
26. Ibid.
27. Ibid., 111–12.
28. Chadwick, "Obituaries: Sir Herbert Butterfield," 6.
29. Butterfield, *The Whig Interpretation*, 115.
30. Ibid., 119–20.
31. Butterfield, *Man on His Past*, 141.
32. Herbert Butterfield, "Sir Edward Grey in July 1914," *Historical Studies: 5—Papers Read Before the Sixth Conference of Irish Historians* (Philadelphia: Dufour Editions, 1965), 1–25; "Crowe's Memorandum of January 1, 1907" (unpublished paper presented at meeting of the British Committee on the Theory of International Politics, July 15–18, 1960), 6–8.
33. Butterfield, *Man on His Past*, 101–3.
34. Ibid., 104.
35. Ibid.
36. Ibid., 106.
37. Ibid., 105.
38. Ibid. Butterfield had little respect for H. G. Wells's *Outline of a History of the World* (1919).
39. Ibid., 107
40. Ibid., 106.
41. Ibid., 112.
42. Ibid., 119–20.
43. Ludwig Dehio, *The Precarious Balance* (New York: Knopf, 1962).
44. Butterfield, *Man on His Past*, 119–20.
45. Ibid., 124.
46. Herbert Butterfield, *Christianity in European History* (London: Oxford University Press, 1951); *The Origins of Modern Science, 1300–1800*, rev. ed. (New York: Macmillan, 1965), 7.
47. Butterfield, *Man on His Past*, 127.
48. Ibid., 127–28. Gertrude Himmelfarb, *Lord Acton* (Chicago: University of Chicago Press, 1952); Jacob Burckhardt, *Reflections on History* (Indianapolis: Liberty Classics, 1979). For a valuable English anthology of Ranke's works, see Leopold von Ranke, *The Theory and Practice of History*, ed. Georg G. Iggers and Konrad von Moltke (New York: Bobbs-Merrill, 1973). See also the interpretative study of Theodore H. von Laue, *Leopold Ranke, the Formative Years* (Princeton, N.J.: Princeton University Press, 1950).
49. The *Scrutiny* article (vol. 1, no. 4, March 1933, pp. 339–55) was reprinted in full in Herbert Butterfield, *History and Human Relations* (London: Collins, 1951).
50. Ibid., 71–72.
51. Ibid., 77–78.

52. Ibid., 79–80.
53. Ibid., 83–84.
54. Ibid., 90, 94.
55. Ibid., 81.
56. Herbert Butterfield, *George III and the Historians*, rev. ed. (New York: Macmillan, 1957), 203, 204.

4 The prophecies of the historian

1. Butterfield, *Christianity and History*, 112.
2. Fyodor Dostoevsky, *The Brothers Karamazov* (New York: Modern Library, 1940); Nikolai Berdyaev, *Slavery and Freedom* (New York: Scribner's, 1944); Alexander Solzhenitsyn, *The Gulag Archipelago*, vol. 2 (New York: Harper & Row, 1975).
3. Butterfield, *Christianity and History*, 95.
4. Herbert Butterfield, *The Englishman and His History* (Cambridge, Eng.: Cambridge University Press, 1944).
5. Butterfield, *Man on His Past*, 106.
6. Butterfield, *Christianity and History*, 94.
7. Ibid., 101–2.
8. Ibid., 102.
9. Ibid., 100.
10. Ibid., 101, 102. Also, notes on "History of Diplomacy" (unpublished).
11. Ibid., 103–4.
12. Ibid., 103.
13. Ibid.
14. Ibid., 103–4.
15. Ibid., 105.
16. Butterfield, *The Englishman and His History*.
17. Ibid.
18. Norman Graebner, "Moralism and American Foreign Policy," and Hans J. Morgenthau, "Human Rights and Foreign Policy," in Kenneth W. Thompson, ed., *Herbert Butterfield: The Ethics of History and Politics* (Washington, D.C.: University Press of America, 1980), 89–98, 99–106.
19. Herbert Butterfield, letter to John Hugh Adam Watson, May 2, 1949 (unpublished).
20. For corroboration of this point, see Arthur A. Stein, *The Nation at War* (Baltimore: Johns Hopkins University Press, 1980), and the review of this book by Davis B. Bobrow, *The American Political Science Review*, vol. 76, no. 1 (March 1982), 203–4. Those who argue in favor of war as a source of moral and spiritual regeneration for a society should consider Thucydides' somber account of the social and moral breakdown in Athens generated by the war against Sparta and the plague.
21. Winston Churchill, *The Gathering Storm* (Boston: Houghton Mifflin, 1948), p. 320.
22. Butterfield, *Christianity and History*, 57.
23. Michael Howard, "Ethics and Power in International Policy," in Kenneth W. Thompson, ed., *Herbert Butterfield: The Ethics of History and Politics*, 57–58.
24. Butterfield, *Christianity and History*, 60.
25. Ibid., 48–50.
26. Peter Geyl, *Encounters in History* (London: Collins, 1963).
27. Butterfield, *Christianity and History*, 52, 62–63.
28. Reinhold Niebuhr, *Faith and History* (New York: Scribner's, 1949), 113.
29. Martin Wight, "The Church, Russia, and the West," *Ecumenical Review*, vol. 1, no. 1 (Autumn 1948), 29.

5   The tragedy of politics and power

1. Herbert Butterfield, *Christianity, Diplomacy and War* (London: Epworth, 1953), 82–83.
2. Fyodor Dostoevsky, *Notes from Underground* (New York: Dutton, 1960), 27.
3. Butterfield, *Christianity and History*, 28–29.
4. Ibid., 45, 31–34.
5. Herbert Butterfield, "Global Good and Evil: I. The Moderate Cupidity of Everyman," *The New York Times* (January 3, 1973), 34.
6. Blaise Pascal, *Pensées*, trans. W. F. Trotter (New York: Dutton, 1958), no. 100.
7. Butterfield, *Christianity and History*, 39–40. Butterfield's strong admiration for Churchill was evident in the memorial address he pronounced at Great Saint Mary's Church on January 31, 1965, on the occasion of the statesman's death. The text can be found in *The Cambridge Review*, vol. 86 (February 6, 1965), 234.
8. Butterfield, *Christianity and History*, 39–40.
9. Ibid., 37–38.
10. Butterfield, *History and Human Relations*, 10.
11. Martin Wight, "The Church, Russia, and the West," 36.
12. Butterfield, *Christianity and History*, 37.
13. Pascal, *Pensées*, nos. 477, 456. See also Herbert Deane, *The Political and Social Ideas of St. Augustine* (New York: Columbia University Press, 1963).
14. Gerhard Ritter, *The Corrupting Influence of Power* (Westport, Conn.: Hyperion Press, 1979), 1.
15. Herbert Butterfield, "History of Diplomacy" (unpublished).
16. Herbert Butterfield, *International Conflict in the Twentieth Century: A Christian View* (New York: Harper & Bros., 1960), 29.
17. Cited in Butterfield, *Christianity, Diplomacy and War*, 56–57.
18. Thomas Hobbes, *Leviathan*, chs. X, XI.
19. Butterfield, *History and Human Relations*, 9–36.
20. Butterfield, "The Moderate Cupidity of Everyman."
21. Friedrich Meinecke, *Machiavellism: The Doctrine of Raison d'État and Its Place in Modern History* (New Haven, Conn.: Yale University Press, 1957), 39.
22. Herbert Butterfield, *The Statecraft of Machiavelli* (New York: Collier, 1962).
23. Ibid., 23–33.
24. Niccolò Machiavelli, *The Prince* (Northbrook, Ill.: AHM Publishing Corp., 1947), 44.
25. Butterfield, *The Statecraft of Machiavelli*, 84, 85.
26. Herbert Butterfield, "Raison d'État: The Relations between Morality and Government," the first Martin Wight Memorial Lecture delivered at the University of Sussex, April 23, 1975; Herbert Butterfield, "Diplomacy," in *Studies in Diplomatic History: Essays in Memory of David Bayne Horn*, ed. Reginald Hatton and M. S. Anderson (Harlow: Longmans, 1970), 357–72, 365.
27. Armand-Jean du Plessis, Duke of Richelieu, *Political Testament*, trans. Henry Bertram Hill (Madison: University of Wisconsin Press, 1961), 101–2.
28. Butterfield, "Diplomacy," 365.
29. Herbert Butterfield, "Religion and Politics" (unpublished).
30. See the relevant discussion of this general theme in Michael Howard, "Ethics and Power in International Policy," in Kenneth W. Thompson, ed., *Herbert Butterfield: The Ethics of History and Politics* (Washington, D.C.: University Press of America, 1980), 62–68.
31. Butterfield, *The Origins of History*, 183–84.
32. It was partly for this reason that Butterfield and Martin Wight tried to limit the participation of government officials in the deliberations of the British Committee on the The-

ory of International Politics. The tendency toward self-justification on the part of those who exercised power could be diffused if the committee was not allowed to become a "statesmen's club."

6   Statesmanship as the search for order

1. Butterfield, *Christianity, Diplomacy and War*, 56–59.
2. Herbert Butterfield, "The Balance of Power," in Herbert Butterfield and Martin Wight, eds., *Diplomatic Investigations* (Cambridge, Mass.: Harvard University Press, 1966), 132–48, 134–36.
3. Ibid., 136–38, 147.
4. Butterfield, "Diplomacy," 369.
5. Ibid., 370.
6. Butterfield, *Christianity, Diplomacy and War*, 68–69.
7. Ibid., 69–70.
8. Butterfield and Wight, *Diplomatic Investigations*; Adam Watson, *Diplomacy: The Dialogue between States* (New York: McGraw-Hill, 1983).
9. Butterfield, "Diplomacy," 364–65.
10. Richelieu, *Political Testament*, 94, 95, 99.
11. Butterfield, *Christianity, Diplomacy and War*, 81. See also Butterfield's comment in *Diplomatic Investigations*, 147: "An international order is not a thing bestowed by nature, but is a matter of refined thought, careful contrivance and elaborate artifice. At best it is a precarious thing, and though it seems so abstract it requires the same kind of loyalty, the same constant attention, that people give to their country or to the other private causes which only the international order enables them to follow."
12. Butterfield, *Christianity, Diplomacy and War*, 76.
13. See pp. 63–64 above.
14. Butterfield, "Comments on Hedley Bull's Paper on the Grotian Conception of International Relations," 12–13.
15. Ibid., 13.
16. Butterfield, *Christianity and History*, 42.
17. Butterfield, "Religion and Politics," 9–10; Butterfield, "Morality and an International Order," 356.

7   Order and politics in the twentieth century

1. Butterfield, *The Origins of History*, 136.
2. Butterfield, "Sir Edward Grey in July 1914," 1–25.
3. Ibid., 3.
4. See "Crowe's Memorandum of January 1, 1907" (unpublished paper presented at the meeting of the British Committee on the Theory of International Politics, July 15–18, 1960).
5. Ibid.
6. Butterfield, "Sir Edward Grey in July 1914," 5.
7. Paul W. Schroeder, "World War I as Galloping Gertie: A Reply to Joachim Remak," *Journal of Modern History*, vol. 44, no. 3 (Sept. 1972), 319–45.
8. Butterfield, *Historical Studies*, 19.
9. Ibid.
10. Ibid., 21.
11. Ibid., 19.

12. Ibid., 20.
13. Ibid.
14. Ibid., 21.
15. Cited in Moorhead Wright, ed., *Theory and Practice of the Balance of Power* (London: Dent, 1975), 136–37.
16. Schroeder, "Galloping Gertie," 345.
17. Butterfield, letter to John Hugh Adam Watson, May 2, 1949 (unpublished).
18. Butterfield, *International Conflict in the Twentieth Century*, 27–38; Butterfield, "Misgivings about the Western Attitude to World Affairs" (unpublished paper presented at a meeting of the British Committee on the Theory of International Politics, January 1959).
19. Adam Watson, "Toleration in Religion and Politics," in Kenneth W. Thompson, ed., *Herbert Butterfield: The Ethics of History and Politics* (Washington, D.C.: University Press of America, 1980), 71–85.
20. Butterfield, "Morality and an International Order," 355.
21. Ibid.
22. Butterfield, *International Conflict in the Twentieth Century*, 97.
23. Ibid., 95–96, 98.
24. Butterfield, "Morality and an International Order," 356.
25. Butterfield, "Religion and Politics," 9–10. Butterfield followed closely Coral Bell's studies on detente and Henry Kissinger's diplomacy in the 1970s. See also John Lewis Gaddis, "The Rise, Fall, and Future of Detente," *Foreign Affairs*, vol. 62, no. 2 (Winter 1983/84), 354–77.
26. Raymond Aron, "The Quest for a Philosophy of Foreign Affairs," in Stanley Hoffmann, ed., *Contemporary Theory in International Relations* (Englewood Cliffs, N.J.: Prentice-Hall, 1960), 79–91.
27. *Parliamentary Debates (Hansard), House of Commons*, vol. 446, no. 48, 562–63, cited in Hans J. Morgenthau, *Politics among Nations*, 5th ed. rev. (New York: Knopf, 1978), 560.
28. Butterfield, "Comments on Hedley Bull's Paper on the Grotian Conception of International Relations," 8.
29. Cowling, "Herbert Butterfield," 606. For a persuasive rebuttal of Butterfield's arguments for unilateral nuclear disarmament, directed at Bertrand Russell, see Stefan T. Possony, *Resistance or Death?: The Perils of Surrender Propaganda* (Bryn Mawr: ISI, 1961).

8   Christianity's challenge to the contemporary world

1. Butterfield, *Christianity in European History*, 10.
2. Butterfield, *International Conflict in the Twentieth Century*, 101–20; *Christianity and History*, 137–46.
3. Butterfield, *Christianity in European History*, 11.
4. Ibid., 17–18.
5. Ibid., 26.
6. Ibid., 28–29.
7. Ibid., 24, 31.
8. Ibid., 34–35.
9. Ibid., 35.
10. Ibid., 52–53.
11. Butterfield, "Religion and Politics," 1.
12. Richelieu, *Political Testament*, 125–26.

13. Butterfield, "Religion and Politics," 11.
14. Reinhold Niebuhr, *The Children of Light and the Children of Darkness* (New York: Scribner's, 1944).
15. Butterfield, "Religion and Politics," 12.
16. Ibid.
17. Ibid., 11.
18. Ibid., 11–12.
19. Ibid., 13.
20. The Lasswell-McDougal international legal jurisprudence and the "world order models" school associated with the names of Richard Falk and Saul Mendlovitz are examples of such efforts, even though (and this may be an indication of their failure to achieve universality) both schools are at odds in many of their *specific* prescriptions.
21. Butterfield, *Christianity in European History*, 55.

9   Butterfield and the quest for political wisdom in international relations

1. See, for example, the discussion in Patrick Gardiner, ed., *Theories of History* (Glencoe, Ill.: Free Press, 1959), 124–87.
2. Herbert Butterfield, "The Role of the Individual in History," *History*, new ser., vol. 40 (Feb. and June 1955), 1–17.
3. Ibid., 3.
4. Ibid., 6.
5. Ibid.
6. Ibid., 7.
7. Ibid., 9, 8.
8. Ibid., 13–14.
9. Ibid., 15–16.
10. See the chapter "The Great Men of History," in Jacob Burckhardt, *Reflections on History* (Indianapolis: Liberty Classics, 1979), 269–315.
11. Herbert Butterfield, "In Memoriam Winston Churchill," *The Cambridge Review*, vol. 86 (February 6, 1965), 234.
12. Ibid.
13. José Ortega y Gasset, *Man and Crisis*, trans. Mildred Adams (New York: Norton, 1958).
14. This is suggested, for example, by Fyodor Dostoevsky in *Notes from Underground*.
15. Butterfield, "Crowe's Memorandum of January 1, 1907," 6–8.
16. Herbert Butterfield, *The Universities and Education Today* (London: Routledge and Kegan Paul, 1962). Burckhardt was of the same opinion. "If history is ever to help us to solve even an infinitesimal part of the great and grievous riddle of life, we must quit the regions of personal and temporal foreboding for a sphere in which our view is not forthwith dimmed by self. It may be that a calmer consideration from a greater distance may yield a first hint of the true nature of life on earth." Burckhardt, *Reflections on History*, 41.
17. For discussions of the problems involved in drawing historical analogies, see the second half of Gardiner, *Theories of History*, and Hans Morgenthau, "Remarks on the Validity of Historical Analogies," *Social Research*, vol. 39, no. 2 (Summer 1972), 360–64.
18. Butterfield, *History and Human Relations*, 181.
19. Michael Howard, "Ethics and Power in International Policy," in Kenneth W. Thompson, ed., *Herbert Butterfield: The Ethics of History and Politics* (Washington, D.C.: University Press of America, 1980), 56.

Bibliography

Primary Sources: Works by Sir Herbert Butterfield

"The Balance of Power" and "The New Diplomacy and Historical Diplomacy." In *Diplomatic Investigations*, edited by Herbert Butterfield and Martin Wight. Cambridge, Mass.: Harvard University Press, 1966.

Charles James Fox and Napoleon: The Peace Negotiations of 1806. Creighton Lecture in History, 1961. London: Athlone Press, 1962.

"The Christian Idea of God." *Listener*, vol. 44, no. 1134 (November 23, 1950), 591, 594.

Christianity and History. New York: Scribner's, 1950.

"Christianity and Politics." *Orbis*, vol. 10, no. 4 (Winter 1967), 1233–46.

Christianity, Diplomacy and War. London: Epworth, 1953.

Christianity in European History. London: Oxford University Press, 1951.

"Christianity in History." *The Dictionary of the History of Ideas*, vol. 1, 373–412. New York: Scribner's, 1973.

"Comments on Hedley Bull's Paper on the Grotian Conception of International Relations." Unpublished paper presented at a meeting of the British Committee on the Theory of International Politics, July 20–23, 1962.

"Crowe's Memorandum of January 1, 1907." Unpublished paper presented at a meeting of the British Committee on the Theory of International Politics, July 15–18, 1960.

"Diplomacy." In *Studies in Diplomatic History: Essays in Memory of David Bayne Horn*, edited by Reginald Hatton and M. S. Anderson, 357–72. Harlow: Longmans, 1970.

The Discontinuities between the Generations in History. Rede Lecture, 1971. London: Cambridge University Press, 1972.

The Englishman and His History. Cambridge, Eng.: Cambridge University Press, 1944.

George III and the Historians. Rev. ed. New York: Macmillan, 1959.

George III, Lord North and the People, 1779–1780. London: G. Bell & Sons, 1949.

"Global Good and Evil: I. The Moderate Cupidity of Everyman." *The New York Times* (January 3, 1973), 33.

Herbert Butterfield: Writings on Christianity and History. Edited by C. T. McIntire. New York: Oxford University Press, 1979.

Historical Development of the Principle of Toleration in British Life. Robert Waley Cohen Memorial Lecture, 1956. London: Epworth Press, 1957.

The Historical Novel: An Essay. Cambridge, Eng.: Cambridge University Press, 1924.

"The Historic States-Systems." Unpublished paper presented at a meeting of the British Committee on the Theory of International Politics, January 8–11, 1965.

"Historiography." *The Dictionary of the History of Ideas*, vol. 2, 464–98. New York: Scribner's, 1973.

History and Human Relations. London: Collins, 1951.

History and Man's Attitude to the Past: Their Role in the History of Civilisation. London: University of London, School of Oriental and African Studies, 1961.

History as the Emancipation from the Past. London: London School of Economics and Political Science, 1956.

"History of Diplomacy." Unpublished paper.

Human Nature and the Dominion of Fear. Christian CND Pamphlet no. 3. London, 1962.

"In Memoriam Winston Churchill." *The Cambridge Review,* vol. 86 (February 6, 1965), 234.

International Conflict in the Twentieth Century: A Christian View. New York: Harper & Bros., 1960.

Letter to John Hugh Adam Watson, May 2, 1949.

Letter to Kenneth W. Thompson, December 10, 1976.

Letter to Kenneth W. Thompson, November 1, 1977.

Liberty in the Modern World. Toronto: Ryerson Press, 1952.

Lord Acton. London: The Historical Association, 1948.

Magna Carta in the Historiography of the Sixteenth and Seventeenth Centuries. Stenton Lecture, 1968. Reading: University of Reading, 1969.

Man on His Past. Cambridge, Eng.: Cambridge University Press, 1955.

"Misgivings about the Western Attitude to World Affairs." Unpublished paper presented at a meeting of the British Committee on the Theory of International Politics, January 1959.

"Morality and an International Order." In *The Aberystwyth Papers: International Politics, 1919–1969,* edited by Brian Porter, 336–57. London: Oxford University Press, 1972.

"My Literary Productions." Unpublished paper.

Napoleon. London: Duckworth, 1939.

The Origins of History. New York: Basic Books, 1981.

The Origins of Modern Science, 1300–1800. Rev. ed. New York: Macmillan, 1965.

The Peace Tactics of Napoleon: 1806–1808. Cambridge, Eng.: Cambridge University Press, 1929.

The Present State of Historical Scholarship: An Inaugural Lecture. Cambridge, Eng.: Cambridge University Press, 1965.

"Protestantism and the Rise of Capitalism." Unpublished paper.

"Raison d'État: The Relations between Morality and Government." First Martin Wight Memorial Lecture delivered at the University of Sussex, April 23, 1975.

The Reconstruction of an Historical Episode: The History of the Enquiry into the Origins of the Seven Years' War. Glasgow University Publications no. 91. Glasgow: Jackson, Son & Co., 1951.

"Reflections on Religion and Modern Individualism." *Journal of the History of Ideas,* vol. 22, no. 1 (Jan.–Mar. 1961), 33–36.

"Religion and Politics." Unpublished paper.

Review: "A. J. P. Taylor on Bismarck." *The Cambridge Review,* vol. 77 (November 5, 1955), 116–19.

Review: "Capitalism and the Rise of Protestantism." *The Cambridge Review,* vol. 63 (May 23, 1942), 324–25.

Review: "Holstein's Memoirs and Historical Criticism." *Encounter,* vol. 5, no. 3 (no. 24, Sept. 1955), 71–79.

"The Role of the Individual in History." *History,* new ser., vol. 40 (Feb. and June 1955), 1–17.

"The Scientific versus the Moralistic Approach in International Affairs." *International Affairs,* vol. 27 (1951), 411–22.

With others. *A Short History of France from Early Times to 1958*, edited by J. Hampden Jackson. Cambridge, Eng.: Cambridge University Press, 1959.

"Sincerity and Insincerity in Charles James Fox." Raleigh Lecture on History, 1971. In *Proceedings of the British Academy*, vol. 57 (1971), 260–87. London: Oxford University Press, 1973.

"Sir Edward Grey in July 1914." In *Historical Studies: 5—Papers Read before the Sixth Conference of Irish Historians*, 1–25. Philadelphia: Dufour Editions, 1965.

The Statecraft of Machiavelli. New York: Macmillan, 1956.

The Study of Modern History: An Inaugural Lecture. London: G. Bell & Sons, 1944.

"Toleration in Early Modern Times." Unpublished paper.

The Universities and Education Today. London: Routledge and Kegan Paul, 1962.

The Whig Interpretation of History. New York: Norton, 1965.

"The Yorkshire Association and the Crisis of 1779–1780." In *Royal Historical Society, London Transactions*, 4th ser., vol. 29, 69–91. London: Royal Historical Society, 1947.

Secondary Sources

Aristotle, *Nichomachean Ethics*. Translated by Martin Oswald. Indianapolis: Bobbs-Merrill, 1962.

———. *Politics*. Edited and translated by Ernest Barker. Oxford: Clarendon Press, 1946.

Aron, Raymond. *Peace and War*. Garden City, N.Y.: Doubleday, 1966.

———. *Politics and History*. New York: Free Press, 1978.

Augustine, Saint. *The Political Writings of St. Augustine*. Edited by Henry Paolucci. South Bend, Ind.: Regnery/Gateway, 1962.

Beitz, Charles R. *Political Theory and International Relations*. Princeton, N.J.: Princeton University Press, 1979.

Berdyaev, Nikolai. *Slavery and Freedom*. New York: Scribner's, 1944.

Bozeman, Adda. *The Future of Law in a Multicultural World*. Princeton, N.J.: Princeton University Press, 1971.

———. "On the Relevance of Hugo Grotius and De Jure Belli ac Pacis for our Times." *Grotiana*, vol. 1 (1980), 65–124.

———. *Politics and Culture in International History*. Princeton, N.J.: Princeton University Press, 1960.

Bull, Hedley. *The Anarchical Society*. New York: Columbia University Press, 1977.

Burckhardt, Jacob. *Reflections on History*. Indianapolis: Liberty Classics, 1979.

Burke, Edmund. *Reflections on the Revolution in France*. Indianapolis: Bobbs-Merrill, 1955.

Callières, François de. *On the Manner of Negotiating with Princes*. Boston: Houghton Mifflin, 1919.

Carr, Edward Hallett. *The Twenty Years' Crisis, 1919–1939*. New York: Harper & Row, 1964.

Churchill, Winston S. *The Second World War*. 6 vols. Boston: Houghton Mifflin, 1948.

Claude, Inis L. *Power and International Relations*. New York: Random House, 1962.

Clausewitz, Carl von. *On War*. Translated from the German by J. J. Graham. Harmondsworth, Eng.: Penguin Books, 1980.

Clive, John. "The Prying Yorkshireman." *New Republic*, vol. 186, no. 25 (June 23, 1982), 31–36.

Cosgrave, Patrick. "An Englishman and His History." *Spectator*, vol. 243 (July 28, 1979), 22–23.

Cowling, Maurice. "Herbert Butterfield: 1900–1979." In *Proceedings of the British Academy*, vol. 65 (1979), 595–609. London: Oxford University Press, 1981.

———. *The Nature and Limits of Political Science*. Cambridge, Eng.: Cambridge University Press, 1963.

———. *Religion and Public Doctrine in Modern England*. Cambridge, Eng.: Cambridge University Press, 1980.

Craig, Gordon. *War, Politics and Diplomacy*. London: Weidenfeld and Nicolson, 1966.

Dawson, Christopher. *The Judgment of the Nations*. New York: Sheed & Ward, 1942.

Deane, Herbert. *The Political and Social Ideas of St. Augustine*. New York: Columbia University Press, 1963.

Dostoevsky, Fyodor. *The Brothers Karamazov*. New York: Modern Library, 1940.

———. *Notes from Underground and the Grand Inquisitor*. New York: Dutton, 1960.

Elliott, J. H., and Koenigsberger, H. G., eds. *The Diversity of History: Essays in Honor of Herbert Butterfield*. London: Routledge and Kegan Paul, 1970.

Falk, Richard A. *A Study of Future Worlds*. New York: Free Press, 1975.

Gaddis, John Lewis. "The Rise, Fall and Future of Detente." *Foreign Affairs*, vol. 62, no. 2 (Winter 1983/84), 354–77.

Gardiner, Patrick, ed. *Theories of History*. Glencoe, Ill.: Free Press, 1959.

Germino, Dante. *Machiavelli to Marx*. Chicago: University of Chicago Press, 1979.

Geyl, Peter. *Encounters in History*. London: Collins, 1963.

Gibbon, Edward. *The Decline and Fall of the Roman Empire*. New York: The Modern Library, 1954.

Goodwin, Geoffrey, ed. *Ethics and Nuclear Deterrence*. New York: St. Martin's, 1982.

Grotius, Hugo. *The Law of War and Peace*. New York: Walter J. Black, 1949.

Hare, J. E., and Joynt, C. B. *Ethics and International Affairs*. New York: St. Martin's, 1982.

Himmelfarb, Gertrude. *Lord Acton*. Chicago: University of Chicago Press, 1962.

Hoffmann, Stanley. *Duties Beyond Borders*. Syracuse: Syracuse University Press, 1981.

———, ed. *Contemporary Theory in International Relations*. Englewood Cliffs, N.J.: Prentice-Hall, 1960.

Howard, Michael. *The Causes of Wars and Other Essays*. Cambridge, Mass.: Harvard University Press, 1983.

Jonas, Hans. "The Practical Uses of Theory." *Social Research*, vol. 26, no. 2 (Summer 1959), 127–66.

Kissinger, Henry. *A World Restored*. New York: Grosset and Dunlap, 1964.

Lafore, Lawrence. *The Long Fuse*. Philadelphia: Lippincott, 1965.

Laue, Theodore H. von. *Leopold Ranke, the Formative Years*. Princeton, N.J.: Princeton University Press, 1950.

Lewis, C. S. *The Abolition of Man*. New York: Macmillan, 1947.

———. *Mere Christianity*. New York: Macmillan, 1952.

Löwith, Karl. *Meaning in History*. Chicago: University of Chicago Press, 1949.

McDougal, Myres S. *Studies in World Public Order*. New Haven, Conn.: Yale University Press, 1960.

Machiavelli, Niccolò. *The Discourses*. Edited by Bernard Crick. Harmondsworth, Eng.: Penguin Books, 1970.

———. *The Prince*. Translated and edited by T. G. Bergin. Northbrook, Ill.: AHM, 1947.

Mackinnon, Donald M. "Power Politics and Religious Faith: The Fifth Martin Wight Memorial Lecture." *British Journal of International Studies*, vol. 6, no. 1 (April 1980), 1–15.

———. "Theology and Tragedy." *Religious Studies*, vol. 2, no. 2 (1966–67), 163–69.

May, Ernest. *"Lessons" of the Past: The Use and Misuse of History in American Foreign Policy*. New York: Oxford University Press, 1975.

Meinecke, Friedrich. *The German Catastrophe*. Boston: Beacon Press, 1963.

———. *Machiavellism: The Doctrine of Raison d'État and Its Place in Modern History*. New Haven, Conn.: Yale University Press, 1957.

Morgenthau, Hans J. *Politics among Nations*. 5th ed. rev. New York: Knopf, 1978.

———. *Scientific Man vs. Power Politics*. Chicago: University of Chicago Press, 1946.

Nardin, Terry. *Law, Morality, and the Relations of States*. Princeton, N.J.: Princeton University Press, 1983.

Nicolson, Harold. *Diplomacy*. 3d ed. Oxford: Oxford University Press, 1973.

Niebuhr, Reinhold. *The Children of Light and the Children of Darkness*. New York: Scribner's, 1944.

———. *Faith and History*. New York: Scribner's, 1949.

———. *The Nature and Destiny of Man*. 2 vols. New York: Scribner's, 1943.

"Obituaries: Sir Herbert Butterfield." *The Cambridge Review* (November 16, 1979), 6–9.

Ortega y Gasset, José. *Man and Crisis*. New York: Norton, 1958.

Osgood, Robert E., and Tucker, Robert W. *Force, Order, and Justice* (Baltimore: Johns Hopkins University Press, 1967).

Pascal, Blaise. *Pensées*. Translated by W. F. Trotter. New York: E. P. Dutton, 1958.

Polybius. *Polybius on Roman Imperialism*. Edited by Alvin H. Bernstein. South Bend, Ind.: Regnery/Gateway, 1980.

Possony, Stefan T. *Resistance or Death?: The Perils of Surrender Propaganda*. Bryn Mawr: ISI, 1961.

Ranke, Leopold von. *The Theory and Practice of History*. Edited by Georg G. Iggers and Konrad von Moltke. New York: Bobbs-Merrill, 1973.

Richelieu, Armand-Jean du Plessis. *The Political Testament*. Translated by Henry Bertram Hill. Madison: University of Wisconsin Press, 1961.

Ritter, Gerhard. *The Corrupting Influence of Power*. Westport, Conn.: Hyperion Press, 1979.

Schmidt, Helmut. "The Morality, Duty and Responsibility of the Politician." *Bulletin*. Bonn: Press and Information Office of the Federal Government, May 26, 1981.

Schroeder, Paul W. "World War I as Galloping Gertie: A Reply to Joachim Remak." *Journal of Modern History*, vol. 44, no. 3 (Sept. 1972), 342–44.

Solzhenitsyn, Alexander. *The Gulag Archipelago*. Vol. 2. New York: Harper & Row, 1975.

Sterling, Richard W. *Ethics in a World of Power*. Princeton, N.J.: Princeton University Press, 1958.

Strauss, Leo. *Natural Right and History*. Chicago: University of Chicago Press, 1953.

Thompson, Kenneth W. *Christian Ethics and the Dilemmas of Foreign Policy*. Durham, N.C.: Duke University Press, 1959.

———. *Masters of International Thought*. Baton Rouge: Louisiana State University Press, 1980.

———. *Morality and Foreign Policy*. Baton Rouge: Louisiana State University Press, 1980.

———. "Toynbee and the Theory of International Politics." *Political Science Quarterly*, vol. 71, no. 3 (Sept. 1956), 365–86.

———. *Winston Churchill's World View*. Baton Rouge: Louisiana State University Press, 1983.

———, ed. *Herbert Butterfield: The Ethics of History and Politics*. Washington, D.C.: University Press of America, 1980.

Thucydides. *History of the Peloponnesian War*. Baltimore, Md.: Penguin Books, 1972.

Tucker, Robert W. *The Inequality of Nations*. New York: Basic Books, 1977.

Unamuno, Miguel de. *Del Sentimiento Tragico de la Vida*. Madrid: Espasa-Calpe, 1967.

Vitoria, Francisco de. *Obras: Relecciones Teologicas*. Madrid: Editorial Catolica, 1960.

Voegelin, Eric. *Order and History*. Vol. 4: *The Ecumenic Age*. Baton Rouge: Louisiana State University Press, 1974.

————. *Science, Politics, and Gnosticism*. Chicago: Regnery, 1968.

Waltz, Kenneth N. *Man, the State, and War*. New York: Columbia University Press, 1959.

Watson, Adam. *Diplomacy: The Dialogue between States*. New York: McGraw-Hill, 1983.

Wight, Martin. "The Church, Russia and the West." *Ecumenical Review*, vol. 1, no. 1 (Autumn 1948), 25–45.

————. *Power Politics*. London: Chatham House, 1946.

————. *Systems of States*. Leicester, Eng.: Leicester University Press, 1977.

Wright, Moorhead, ed. *Theory and Practice of the Balance of Power*. London: Dent, 1975.

Index